on track ...

Carpenters

every album, every song

Paul Tornbohm

sonicbondpublishing.com

Sonicbond Publishing Limited
www.sonicbondpublishing.co.uk
Email: info@sonicbondpublishing.co.uk

First Published in the United Kingdom 2023
First Published in the United States 2023

British Library Cataloguing in Publication Data:
A Catalogue record for this book is available from the British Library

Typeset in ITC Garamond Std & ITC Avant Garde Gothic
Printed and bound in England

Graphic design and typesetting: Full Moon Media

Follow us on social media:
Twitter: https://twitter.com/SonicbondP
Instagram: www.instagram.com/sonicbondpublishing_/
Facebook: www.facebook.com/SonicbondPublishing/

Linktree QR code:

on track ...

Carpenters

every album, every song

Paul Tornbohm

sonicbondpublishing.com

Dedication
To my mother, Yvonne Hamilton, 1943-2023

Acknowledgements

In researching this book, I am grateful to Carpenters authors Ray Coleman, Mike Cidoni Lennox, Rick Henry, Chris May, John Tobler and Randy L. Schmidt for their detailed research. I am also grateful to those who have shared their knowledge and collections online – including A&M Corner's Carpenters Complete Recording Resource, The Carpenters: History and News Facebook page, Jonathan Owen's online collection, David Grant's discography, and last but definitely not least, Richard Carpenter's official Carpenters website. Chart positions were principally sourced from Craig Halstead's book on the band's Top 40 hits.

I would like to thank Stephen Lambe for this opportunity, my wife Yumi Mashiki for her patience, my sister Cathy for being my Karen Carpenter, and my parents Noel and Yvonne for a musical education. Special thanks to *On Track* authors Peter Kearns, Richard James and Georg Purvis for their helpful guidance.

I am also indebted to the following for their insights and encouragement – Elizabeth Benitez Morales, Tom Bromley, Kevin Chambers (for road-testing Carpenters' cover songs at open-mic nights together), Glen Johnson, Paul Sarcich, Jeremy Simmonds, Royston Vince, Stephen Wang, Matthew Welton, and lastly to my supportive work colleagues.

Foreword

Growing up in the 1970s, our kitchen radio was permanently tuned to the easy-listening station BBC Radio 2, and the group I remember hearing the most was the Carpenters. I also remember seeing the 'Please Mr Postman' video on TV, no doubt because it was filmed at Disneyland: the place in the world I most wanted to visit.

By the time I was a teenager in the 1980s, my musical taste had outgrown Radio 2, but my yesterday-once-more moment came in the 1990s with the release of the tribute album *If I Were A Carpenter*. Here, the alternative rock bands I was listening to (like Sonic Youth and Babes in Toyland) had given the Carpenters' sound a fuzz-and-feedback makeover, and instead of being an ironic takedown of the duo's soft-rocking music, their interpretations sounded surprisingly reverential, proving that deeply melancholic songs like 'Rainy Days and Mondays' and 'Superstar' could resonate with Gen X.

Tragically, Karen Carpenter passed away in 1983. Since then, the Carpenters' story has been retold through books, documentaries and biopics. Their catalogue has been remastered and repackaged, reinterpreted with orchestras, and recreated by tribute acts and artificial intelligence software. The internet has strengthened and increased their fan base from the US and UK to Asia, Latin America and beyond.

To understand their wide-reaching and enduring appeal, I will investigate how the brother-and-sister team created their singular sound, balancing musical sophistication and pop success. I will explore how they drew on diverse influences from jazz and classical to country and pop, and how they chose some of the best musicians, songwriters and studios to realise their unique musical vision. I will review all their studio albums, live and solo releases. Each chapter will begin with insights into an album's making, along with the factors that influenced their success. My main focus is on their music, so I have limited details of their personal lives to the specific events that most directly affected their careers. For anyone seeking further biographical insight, I highly recommend Randy Schmidt's thorough biography *Little Girl Blue: The Life of Karen Carpenter*, Lucy O'Brien's *Lead Sister: The Story of Karen Carpenter*, and other informative books listed in the bibliography. Lastly, I've used some music terminology that may be unfamiliar to some readers but have attempted to contextualise this as much as possible.

on track ...

Carpenters

Contents

Introduction – From The Top 11
Offering/Ticket To Ride (1969) 13
Close To You (1970) 23
Carpenters (Tan album) (1971) 33
A Song For You (1972) 41
Now And Then (1973) 51
Horizon (1975) 61
A Kind Of Hush (1976) 68
Passage (1977) 76
Christmas Portrait (1978) 88
Made In America (1981) 101
Voice Of The Heart (1983) 108
An Old-Fashioned Christmas (1984) 113
Live Albums and Bootlegs 119
Bootlegs 120
Compilations and Tribute Albums 122
Solo Albums and Reinterpretations 130
On Karen's Voice 134
Selected Bibliography 136

Introduction – From The Top

The Carpenter siblings (Richard (b. 15 Oct 1946) and Karen (b. 2 March 1950 – d. 4 Feb 1983) grew up in New Haven, Connecticut, USA. As children, they listened to their father Harold's record collection, which ranged from jazz to western swing, and from piano concertos to traditional Hawaiian music. The pioneering multitrack recordings of guitarist Les Paul and his vocalist wife, Mary Ford, held a particular fascination, as did those by madcap musical comedian Spike Jones. The Carpenter siblings also heard their mother, Agnes, sing along to crooners like Bing Crosby, Perry Como and Nat King Cole on the radio. Both siblings started piano lessons, but gave up within a year, though Richard continued to work out songs by ear on the piano, while Karen was more interested in playing sports and attending dance classes. Richard eventually resumed piano lessons with a new teacher who introduced him to the fake book of jazz chord charts, and who helped him enrol in a weekly piano class at the Yale music school.

At the age of 15, Richard formed a jazz quartet with some High School classmates, which brought his talents to the attention of a group of older musicians. This led to gigs in clubs and restaurants, where Richard hoped the glasses he wore would disguise his true age. It also led to his first recording date, travelling to Manhattan to add Jerry Lee Lewis-style keyboard sweeps to the track 'Why Don't You Write Me' by the New Haven vocal group The Barries. In 1963, when Karen was 13 and Richard 16, the family headed west from Connecticut to California, seeking warmer weather and opportunities for Richard in show business. Spotted at a talent show in a local park, Richard was soon recruited as a church organist, learning to play the pipe organ and sneaking in Beatles tunes alongside the hymns. A local paper ran a story on Richard, which led to an offer from a band in need of a pianist. During his time with this group, Richard met singer Ed Sulzer, who would become the duo's first manager, supporting them through their early incarnations and helping them land their deal with A&M Records.

By the time that group fizzled out, Richard had joined the school concert band, with additional weekend club gigs backing band leader Bruce Gifford in a cabaret group. By 1964, Karen had joined the school marching band on glockenspiel, but her heart was really set on the drums. She began lessons, and even rehearsed briefly with an all-girl instrumental surf band, playing a set that included Beatles numbers. By 1965, and with a Ludwig kit just like Ringo Starr's, Karen was ready to join Richard in The Richard Carpenter Trio: a jazz group formed with another college student, Wes Jacobs. Jacobs was a tuba and double-bass player whom Richard met after starting as a music major at California State University, Long Beach (CSULB). Rehearsing at the Carpenter home, Karen tried singing a few numbers, including 'I Who Have Nothing' and a ballad version of The Beatles' 'I Want to Hold Your Hand'. Unhappy with how she sounded on tape, she quickly retreated back behind the drum kit, and the trio played weddings and dances with a hired singer instead. But in May 1966, Karen followed Richard to a friend's audition for the new independent label Magic Lamp. Karen was invited to give a vocal audition of her own and sang the recent Righteous Brothers hit 'Ebb Tide'. All agreed that her voice had great promise, and she was promptly signed as a solo artist with Richard as her composer/arranger/keyboardist. The studio they visited that night was in the garage of the record label co-founder Joe Osborn: an experienced session bass player and member of L.A.'s legendary Wrecking Crew. Osborn was to give the duo considerable support throughout their career.

The following month, The Richard Carpenter Trio won the Hollywood Bowl Battle of the Bands. They were spotted that day by an RCA Victor talent scout, and were offered a recording contract. They duly recorded demos at RCA studios, but on hearing these, the label obviously thought twice about the prospects of a jazz-rock tuba group, and decided to pass.

By this time, Richard was a member of the CSULB choir, and was learning choral arrangement under its leader, Frank Pooler. Pooler introduced Richard to student and lyricist John Bettis, and the pair became fast friends, working the summer of '67 as vaudeville-era musicians at Coke Corner in Disneyland. Back at university, they gathered other choir members to form the group Summerchimes, who soon evolved into Spectrum. Karen sang and drummed with these groups, and enrolled at the university in 1967, joining the choir. Ed Sulzer touted Spectrum's demo tapes around record labels, and secured them some gigs – most notably as an ill-matched opening act for Steppenwolf – whilst the band often queued up for Hootenanny talent nights on Mondays at West Hollywood's Troubadour. However, the band's old-fashioned choral sound and dowdy image failed to engage the Whisky à Go Go audience, and the band never made it past the first night of their three-night booking. Similarly, their demo tape was provoking more bemusement than interest from record labels. Even offers from two independent labels – Uni and White Whale – ran aground.

When both Spectrum and the Magic Lamp label burnt out, Karen and Richard resolved to present themselves as a duo. To name the band, they chose their surname, leaving out the definite article 'The', as Richard felt this sounded more hip. Throughout 1968, they demoed songs in Joe Osborn's 4-track studio, exploring ways to multitrack their harmonies, and creating the demo that – with Ed Sulzer's help – was to get them signed to A&M Records in 1969.

Offering/Ticket To Ride (1969)

Personnel:
Karen Carpenter: vocals, drums, bass (5, 11)
Richard Carpenter: vocals, keyboards, arranger
Joe Osborn, Bob Messenger: bass
Gary Sims: guitar
Herb Alpert: shaker
Recorded at A&M Records, Hollywood, California
Produced by Jack Daugherty
Engineered by Ray Gerhardt
Release date: 9 October 1969
Charts: US: 150, UK: 20 (1972)
Label: A&M
Retitled *Ticket To Ride*, 10 November 1970
Running time 36:52

After all those years of preparation, when the offer of a recording contract finally arrived, Karen and Richard had just agreed to an advertising deal with the Ford Motor Company, who were to pay the duo $50,000 each and give them each their own Ford Mustang car. Extracting themselves from that deal, the duo signed with A&M on 22 April 1969. One week later, the Carpenters entered studio A on the A&M lot to begin recording their debut album. In their excitement, they gave no thought to changing any of the repertoire they'd developed over the past few years, which was already sounding out-of-date. All the same, the album had high production values, and contained an ambitious blend of jazz and pop, with even a touch of psychedelia. Since Karen preferred her role as drummer and still lacked confidence as a lead singer, she and Richard shared the lead vocals.

As an unknown act, there was less pressure to deliver the album quickly, and they spent the next few months and a generous budget piecing together the elements of what would become their trademark sound. Karen played bass on two numbers, with the remaining bass parts supplied by either Magic Lamp's Joe Osborn or Bob Messenger, whom Richard had met when standing in for another pianist at a gig in Downey, CA. Messenger – a multi-instrumentalist who also played saxophone and flute, was to become a fixture of the duo's touring band.

Richard played the studio's Steinway model A grand piano on tracks like 'Someday', 'Ticket To Ride' and 'Eve'. Elsewhere, he played a harpsichord and the Wurlitzer 140B organ he'd purchased from Jeff Hanna of The Nitty Gritty Dirt Band. Guitarist Gary Sims – another college friend who'd been a member of Summerchimes and Spectrum – played on 'All of My Life' and 'Nowadays Clancy Can't Even Sing'. The album was produced by former Woody Herman Band trumpeter Jack Daugherty, who'd helped forward the Carpenters' demo to A&M's Herb Alpert.

To show off Karen's voice to its fullest, Richard arranged songs to emphasise the lower end of her vocal range with its characterful warmth and tone. He was also mindful to leave space for Karen's vocals when creating orchestral arrangements, reserving the opening verse of ballads for voice and keyboards before introducing other musical elements. He also paired Karen's voice with the near-human tone of reed instruments like the cor anglais and oboe, as heard towards the end of 'Someday'. And right at the heart of their sound were the multitracked vocal harmonies, which the pair would record and then review, deciding whether a part needed to be doubled or tripled.

The ingredients of the Carpenters' unique sound were now in place, yet their debut was still subtly different from their later releases – not only in the pair's shared lead vocals, but in the husky tone of Karen's youthful voice. Several of the lyrics were aligned with the late-1960s countercultural hippy worldview; not that the rock press were persuaded, however, dismissing the duo as little more than a wholesome brother-and-sister vocal act. It also didn't help that the label had placed dull photos of the pair on the front and back of *Offering*. Unsurprisingly, sales were poor, and the album made a loss on its $50,000 production costs. Thankfully, their luck was about to change.

'Invocation' (Richard Carpenter, John Bettis)

Side one begins with a religious *a cappella* pastiche with a lyric stating the album title, *Offering*. This hymn-like piece shows the influence of the Carpenters' choral training under Frank Pooler. The lines are delivered in suitably chorister-like tones, while the arrangement uses techniques like antiphony and call-and-response. Richard described the multilayered choir as an excuse to have fun with voice overdubbing.

The album version is a remix of the demo recorded the previous year by Joe Osborn in his garage studio. This demo, like many of their earliest recordings mentioned throughout this chapter, can be heard in the box-set compilations *From the Top* and *The Essential Collection: 1965-1997*.

'Your Wonderful Parade' (Richard Carpenter, John Bettis)

This recording, made in 1968 in Joe Osborn's garage, was on the demo tape that secured the A&M deal. Some new features were added to the demo for album inclusion, such as the string section, tubular bells and the spoken introduction. Richard also replaced his original lead vocal with a more enthusiastic take, which, together with the upbeat tempo, makes it a strong choice to open the album. Listeners can compare the changes with the original demo available on the compilations mentioned above.

The song was written in 1967 as a youthful satire on the establishment, 'of which we were later to become a part', Richard conceded in the *From the Top* booklet. The lyric makes an absurdist analogy between the routines of a conventional lifestyle and a circus parade march, as depicted by Karen's military drum patterns, which she doubtlessly picked up during her time in the Downey High School marching band. The spoken introduction, therefore, features Richard as a circus barker, recalling Harry Nilsson's announcements at the start of his 1967 *Pandemonium Shadow Show* album, and The Beatles' 'Being for the Benefit of Mr Kite' on *Sgt. Pepper's* ... the same year. The segment closes with a line adapted from Abraham Lincoln's famous 1863 Gettysburg address – 'of the people, by the people and for the people', after which Karen's spoken count-in can be heard.

Musically, the song is full of details, such as Joe Osborn's bass climbing up into the higher register in the middle section to leave space for the cello solo. Also, while the song is in a 4/4 time signature, a sneaky bar of 2/4 is fitted into the bridge section at the phrase 'a better way to fall'. There are also three key changes which can be heard at the start of the verses and cello solo.

To end the song, Karen's military snare drum marches off into the distance with a swirly phase effect applied on top. According to Richard, this was an unintended but welcome by-product that occurred at the album's mastering stage. A similar phase effect can be briefly heard around the two-minute mark on the line 'Meet your wife at cocktail time'.

The song also appeared on the B-side of 'Ticket To Ride' with a newly recorded shorter vocal introduction.

'Someday' (Richard Carpenter, John Bettis)
At 5:13 in length, 'Someday' is the album's longest track and possibly its most epic. From the eerie piano fade-in to the cinematic string sweeps, the arrangement was constructed as a dramatic frame for Karen's passionate performance. This is the album's one track without backing vocals, highlighting the affecting vulnerability in Karen's voice. Whenever she sings the title, the two notes fall by either a 3rd or a 5th, replicating a sigh of exasperation. At the end, the phrase rises instead, as if Karen were proclaiming a powerful promise.

The young couple's fate remains undecided at the song's conclusion, just as Richard's melody lines remain unresolved at the end of each verse, and the brass section plays an unresolved chord at the very end.

The track is a true album high point, though neither Richard nor Karen were fully happy with the recording. Richard was specifically unhappy with the harp distortion in verse two, while Karen was displeased with her vocal, having had a cold on the day of recording. The opportunity to re-record the song came much later when it was revisited in a medley on their 1980 TV special *Music Music Music*. This version can be heard as part of the '1980 Medley' on the *From the Top* and *Essential Collection* compilations.

'Get Together' (Chet Powers)
This era-defining anthem to peace and brotherhood was written by Chet Powers, aka Dino Valenti of Quicksilver Messenger Service, and was first released as 'Let's Get Together' by the Kingston Trio in 1964. Epitomising hippy

ideals, it became a popular track to cover in the 1960s, with versions by artists like Jefferson Airplane, Julie Felix and The Sunshine Company. 'Get Together' is perhaps most associated with The Youngbloods, whose recording inspired Richard to create his own arrangement. But any hopes that the Carpenters may have nurtured of scoring their own hit with the song, were dashed when The Youngbloods' re-released their version in September 1969, hitting five on the *Billboard* Hot 100 just a month before the release of *Offering*.

Trombones were added to the Carpenters' recording at the suggestion of Herb Alpert to give the track more impact. Richard also wanted a psychedelic effect on the vocals, feeding them through his Baldwin keyboard amplifier on the tremolo setting. This may have been inspired by the similar effect on The Beatles' 1966 recording 'Tomorrow Never Knows', where a revolving Leslie speaker was used to alter John Lennon's vocal to sound like the chanting of Tibetan monks on a mountaintop.

'All Of My Life' (Richard Carpenter)

Karen and Richard first recorded this song with Spectrum in 1967, and though that version has never been released, it's currently available online. They recorded another version for the Joe Osborn demo tape, but the version on *Offering/Ticket To Ride* was newly recorded and featured additional orchestration. The yearning lyric is set to a 12/8 rhythm, and recalls 1960s teen ballads like The Angels' 'Cry Baby Cry' or Skeeter Davis' 'The End of the World'. Gary Sims' tremolo guitar also recalls The Beach Boys' 'In My Room': another 12/8 ballad from the 1960s.

Karen's delivery becomes increasingly impassioned towards the song's climax, where the rhythm temporarily changes time signature for three bars of 4/4, before slowing to a pause and returning to 12/8. In addition to drums, Karen also played bass on this song, using an instrument given to her by Joe Osborn. In 1987, he replaced her bass part for the version heard in *The Karen Carpenter Story* (CBS, 1989) and subsequent compilations. Richard also re-recorded his Wurlitzer 140B organ part on a Yamaha DX7 synthesizer.

'Turn Away' (Richard Carpenter, John Bettis)

This cheerful number closes side one and features Richard on vocals. Following an uptempo verse with a funky drum part, the pace slows for the chorus, where backing vocals enter and the key shifts temporarily from D major to B major.

'Ticket To Ride' (John Lennon, Paul McCartney)

Single A-side b/w 'Your Wonderful Parade'
Release date: 5 November 1969
Charts: US: 54

Side two opens with this inventive take on the well-known 1965 Beatles hit. Karen and Richard were both big Beatles fans, playing several of the band's songs in the early repertoire, often giving the pieces a new twist. In this case, the original song's hypnotic, proto-psychedelic mood is reshaped into a dramatic Walker Brothers-style ballad. Karen even seems to mimic Scott Walker's baritone as she drops to the lowest part of her vocal range at the end of each chorus. Many Carpenters recordings were arranged to showcase Karen's characterful lower vocal range, of which (according to Tom Bahler quoted in Ray Coleman's biography) Karen would say, 'The money's in the basement'.

In addition to slowing the tempo, Richard makes further bold modifications to the song, replacing the original intro's hypnotic chiming guitars with a newly-composed classical piano passage. This piano section was included on the album version, but removed for the single release. In the final section of the Beatles recording, the tempo suddenly switches to double time for the repeating line 'My baby don't care', but Richard takes the arrangement in the opposite direction, repeating the phrase 'Think I'm gonna be sad'. Karen and Richard created a four-part harmony for this final line, with the chord's lowest and highest notes pitched at an interval of a 6th apart. They recorded the two outer harmonies first before the inner chord harmonies and then repeated each part a further three times to create a 12-voice *choir*.

The song became their debut single, following the strategy of introducing an unknown act with their recording of a well-known song: in this case, it was a startling reinvention of a Beatles classic. Unfortunately, it was only a moderate hit, climbing slowly to 54 over six months, and reaching 19 on *Billboard*'s Easy Listening chart. A film clip was shot in Squaw Valley, California on 2 March 1970 (Karen's 20th birthday) for the TV show *Something Else*. The snow-filled winter setting recalled The Beatles' filmed performance of the song in the 1965 movie *Help!*, which was filmed on the ski slopes of Obertauern in Austria.

'Don't Be Afraid' (Richard Carpenter)

Picking up the mood, this jaunty ditty instantly demands your attention with a harmonised vocal introduction that pre-empts the iconic backing vocal 'aah's of 'Goodbye To Love' by a few years. With 'Don't Be Afraid', Richard proves he can single-handedly compose a catchy pop tune, though the far-out 1960s lyric sounds very much of its time. Nevertheless, the song appeared in their live sets right up until 1978.

Karen's tone is friendly and reassuring as she delivers the pep talk, yet the amount of reverb on her vocal makes it sound more distant than the backing vocals. Richard's brief keyboard solo concludes with some fast and frantic passages – the result of slowing down the tape to record the complex phrases at an easier speed. The track ends with a cascading vocal canon – a musical device they were to re-employ in future arrangements such as the Bacharach/ David medley.

'Don't Be Afraid' was one of the songs on the original demo tape, and changed little when re-recorded for the *Offering* album.

'What's The Use' (Richard Carpenter, John Bettis)
Another happy-go-lucky number, this was written in the Spectrum days. Richard sings the lead, delivering an ode to being idle that seemingly contradicts his reputation for being hardworking.

The chorus lyric includes a reference to 'I've Got Plenty of Nothing' from George Gershwin's 1935 musical *Porgy and Bess*. Also in the chorus, the line 'I've a better life in mind' can just be heard beneath 'To be somebody's slave for a dime'. The ending breaks down to a simple hi-hat pulse that seems like a count-in to the next song ...

'All I Can Do' (Richard Carpenter, John Bettis)
...except, just to wrong-foot us, this song is in an entirely different time signature – 5/4 and is much faster, almost going past in a blur. Karen demonstrates her impressive drumming, creating a busy, jazz-influenced pattern packed with rapid rolls. Richard's brief Wurlitzer electric piano solo squeezes a lot of notes into a short space, while the deep keyboard bass riff is reminiscent of The Doors. The backing vocal parts combine to form jazz-sounding 9th chords, and the Carpenters acknowledged in interviews how they sang a lot harder in their early career, which can certainly be heard here. In addition to the uncommon 5/4 signature, the verse chords shift unexpectedly up and down by a semitone, passing through two different keys in the chorus.

One of the first Carpenter/Bettis collaborations, this song was originally demoed for Spectrum in 1967 on Richard's two-track reel-to-reel at the Carpenter's home, where vocals were recorded in the bathroom for its unique reverberation. That version can be heard on later compilations. The following year, the duo recorded a new version in Joe Osborn's garage, which was included on the demo heard by Herb Alpert, and remixed for inclusion on *Offering/Ticket To Ride*.

'Eve' (Richard Carpenter, John Bettis)
The tempo now slows for a haunting ballad inspired by a 1968 episode of *Journey to the Unknown*: a British fantasy TV series similar to *The Twilight Zone*. The episode is about the doomed love affair between a sales assistant (played by Dennis Waterman) and a shop mannequin, which occasionally comes to life (played by Carol Lynley).

As with many of the group's ballads, the arrangement begins simply with vocals and piano, before the arrival of bass and drums, both played by Karen. Reflecting the strange story and its unhappy characters, the song's key centre never seems to fully settle, moving erratically in the opening verse, just as a bar of 3/4 disrupts the rhythm at the end of the first line. There is some effective word painting with the line 'Notice how her image saddens', the chord falling from Bb to A-diminished, matching Eve's feeling of dejection.

As with other tracks on the album, Karen was unhappy with her vocal, and planned to re-record it. In particular, she wanted to fix an off-key note on the word 'become' in the second chorus. Though that re-recording never happened, the track was remixed in 1987 with Joe Osborn replacing Karen's bass part, as heard on subsequent compilations.

'Nowadays Clancy Can't Even Sing' (Neil Young)
Perhaps the album's most out-there of the selection, this Neil Young song was first recorded in 1966 by Buffalo Springfield, then covered by psychedelic rock group Fever Tree in 1968. The Clancy of the title was a child Young knew at school, who suffered from multiple sclerosis and also had the habit of singing to himself. Clancy dropped his singing habit after other students mocked him for it, which had saddened and angered Young.

The structure switches from major-key verses in 4/4, to minor-key choruses in 3/4. This version is certainly more spirited than the previous recordings mentioned, adding new backing vocal parts, orchestral and an instrumental coda in 3/4 where Richard plays a long keyboard solo and Karen stretches out on the drums. The song has enough twists and turns to complement the album's other tracks, but few other songs in their catalogue would have lines as strange as 'Who's that stomping all over my face?' or 'Who's seeing eyes through the cracks in the floor?'.

If anything, the song demonstrates how the duo used their debut album to experiment in their search for a musical identity, and Richard has remarked on how little stylistic guidance he received from the record label or management at the time. In interviews, Richard often professed to be a fan of the very singular Frank Zappa, and it's interesting to consider the possible directions the band could've headed in.

'Benediction' (Richard Carpenter, John Bettis)
In religious services, a benediction is a short blessing by which the proceedings are concluded and the congregation is dismissed. This companion piece to 'Invocation' lasts just 40 seconds, has only four lyric lines, and ends again with the album's title *Offering*. Like 'Invocation', it begins with *a cappella* choral harmonies, using semi-religious language to 'offer' the gift of music. A harp glissando launches a powerful blast of tubular bells and strings, and thus, concludes the album.

Related Tracks
'Caravan' (Irving Mills, Duke Ellington)
This energetic version of the 1930 Duke Ellington jazz classic was recorded in the summer of 1965 on Richard's Sony reel-to-reel machine in the family's front room. Calling themselves The Richard Carpenter Trio, they teamed

up with Richard's high-school friend Wes Jacobs on double bass and tuba, and assembled a repertoire of instrumental numbers. Richard created the fast-paced arrangement, giving each player an opportunity to show off their fledgling skills.

After racing through the familiar main melody, the band drops to a swinging, cool-jazz rhythm, where the piano and bass trade bars with the drums. They then move to a 12-bar blues form for Richard's piano solo, which is filled with blues licks and rapid runs up and down the keys. Next comes Jacobs' bass solo, the pace then quickening for Karen's drum solo in which she works her way around the kit in a steady flurry of semiquavers. Returning to the main riff, Richard is heard to shoosh the band towards the end.

Richard was 18 at the time, while Karen was 15 and had been learning drums for only a few months. She can be heard breaking out in excited giggles throughout the recording, along with sneezing at the start.

'Iced Tea' (Richard Carpenter)

In the summer of 1966, the Richard Carpenter Trio played two songs at the Battle of the Bands finals at the Hollywood Bowl – an instrumental version of 'The Girl from Ipanema', and 'Iced Tea': a frantic Richard original written especially for the competition. This piece was designed to show off each band member's skills, including Wes Jacobs on the tuba.

After a frantic introduction, Richard plays a crazed chromatic melody, followed by a scurrying solo of blues licks to a hectic 3/4 rhythm. This is contrasted by a wistful interlude throughout which Jacobs plays a discordant riff using a bow on the double bass. Karen then bursts in with some furious drum fills, pulling us back to the frenzy of the main tune. The band's novelty and skill enabled them to walk away with the winning trophy.

Better yet, as he returned to the car park, Richard was approached by RCA producer Neely Plumb, who arranged for the trio to sign a recording contract. They then made a demo for RCA of eleven instrumentals, including 'Strangers in the Night', The Beatles' 'Every Little Thing', 'I've Never Been in Love Before' from the musical *Guys and Dolls*, and Richard's original numbers 'Iced Tea', 'Flat Baroque' and 'I Never Had a Love Before'. Unfortunately, on hearing the demos, RCA decided not to continue with the band, and the contract was terminated. Of the tracks recorded, 'Iced Tea' is the only one that's been released, and can be found on compilations, while some of the other tracks have found their way onto the internet.

'The Parting Of Our Ways' (Richard Carpenter)

In May 1966, Karen was signed to Magic Lamp Records as a solo artist, only two months after her 16th birthday. Her mother, Agnes, was incensed that the label had overlooked Richard, who she considered to be the more talented of her two children. In a conciliatory move, the label subsequently signed him as a songwriter with the label's publishing wing Lightup Music.

Using the facilities at Joe Osborn's garage, 'The Parting of Our Ways' was one of the first songs Karen recorded as a lead singer, also adding a harmony part and playing drums. Richard plays various keyboards, including the Chamberlin Music Master (a version of the Mellotron) to provide the flute sound. Joe Osborn produced, engineered and played bass.

Richard's song included several twists and turns, from key changes in the bridge and outro to the minor-key song ending unexpectedly on a major chord. Since the song was never a single, and the original master tape was lost in a fire at Osborn's house in 1975, the recording source for these compilations was an acetate reference disc.

'Looking For Love' (Richard Carpenter)
A-side b/w 'I'll Be Yours', issued under the name Karen Carpenter.
This was released in 1966 on the Magic Lamp label, though only around 500 discs were ever issued, making existing copies highly collectable. The source for the *From the Top* compilation was a copy of the single, since the master tape was lost in the 1975 fire.

Many consider this to be the first Carpenters single. The track begins with a catchy piano riff and keyboard flute part, both of which return to close the song. Karen is just 16 years old but sings with authority, adding harmonies and playing a busy drum part. Bass duties are undertaken by Wes Jacobs.

'I'll Be Yours' (Richard Carpenter)
Appearing as the B-side of 'Looking for Love' in 1966, several friends apparently advised the duo that this cheerful number would've made the better A-side. It starts with Karen's drums and a chord progression that's eerily prescient of their later hit 'Sing'. Karen sings lead and backing on this girl-group-style number. The lineup is the same as the other Magic Lamp recordings, though apparently, both Wes Jacobs and Joe Osborn played bass according to the accompanying notes for the track on the *From the Top* and *The Essential Collection: 1965-1997* compilations.

'Nowhere Man' (John Lennon, Paul McCartney)
Originally recorded in 1967 as a demo for Magic Lamp, this track was rearranged and given additional overdubs in 1999 for the compilation *As Time Goes By*. At the time of recording, Karen sang to a simple piano accompaniment, bringing a mature interpretation to the downbeat lyric that many had considered to be a self-reflective John Lennon commentary. For the 1999 arrangement, Richard revised his original basic piano introduction, and added harmonica, bass, oboe and strings.

'You'll Love Me' (Richard Carpenter)
This early demo stands out for its chiming Byrdsian guitar part and male backing vocals. It was one of nine songs recorded at United Audio in Santa

Ana, Orange County, in May 1967 with Summerchimes, who later became the vocal group Spectrum. The lineup here features Karen and Richard in their usual roles, joined by guitarists Gary Sims and John Bettis, and bassist Danny Woodhams. Though this band was short-lived, the members all played a part in the duo's future.

'California Dreaming' (John Phillips, Michelle Phillips)
This song is best known from the hit 1965 version by The Mamas & the Papas, written in 1963 as the writers struggled through a harsh New York winter. The Carpenters recorded their version at Joe Osborn's garage studio, though sources differ as to whether it was 1967 or 1968. Osborn had, in fact, been the bassist on the original Mamas & Papas version, though college friend Bill Siisyoev plays bass on this demo.

Richard decided to replace the entire backing track for the rarities compilation *As Time Goes By*. One of his first moves was to substitute real strings for the part he'd played on a Chamberlin (a precursor of the Mellotron). His busy electric piano solo takes the place of Bud Shank's memorable alto flute solo in The Mamas & Papas version.

'Good Night' (John Lennon, Paul McCartney)
John Lennon originally wrote this affectionate lullaby for his five-year-old son Julian. Ringo Starr sang it as the closing track on The Beatles' *White Album* in 1968. The Carpenters' version was issued on a 1969 album by the CSULB choir. The choir had released an album on the local Young label every year since 1962. Richard contributed piano to the traditional spiritual 'Ain't Got Time to Die' on their 1968 album.

On 9 May 1969, the Carpenters joined Pooler and the choir at Radio Recorders in Los Angeles to record Richard's arrangements of 'Good Night', 'Crescent Noon' and Laura Nyro's gospel number 'And When I Die'. On Nyro's song, Karen sings in a forceful gospel style, sharing the lead vocal with Wanda Freeman, whom Richard accompanies on a further three songs on the album.

Returning to 'Good Night', Richard's choral arrangements differ slightly in style from the parts George Martin scored for the Beatles recordings, showing the influence of Judd 'Jud' Conlon: a vocal arranger Richard admired. In the 1940s and 1950s, Conlon had arranged harmonies for Bing Crosby's vocal backing group The Rhythmaires, and wrote vocal parts for the Walt Disney movies *Alice in Wonderland* and *Peter Pan*. 'Good Night' is included on the compilation *From the Top*. The other songs featuring Karen and the choir have been shared online.

Close To You (1970)

Personnel:
Karen Carpenter: vocals, drums
Richard Carpenter: vocals, keyboards, orchestrator, arranger
Joe Osborn, Danny Woodhams: bass
Jim Horn, Doug Strawn, Bob Messenger: woodwinds
Hal Blaine: drums
Produced by Jack Daugherty
Engineered by Ray Gerhardt and Dick Bogert
Recorded at A&M Records, Hollywood, California
Release date: 9 August 1970
Label: A&M
Charts: US: 2, UK: 23 (1973)
Running Time 38:37

As their first single made only a modest chart impact and album sales had failed to recoup costs, the duo might've worried that A&M might drop them. Fortunately, Herb Alpert still believed in them, and replaced their manager, Ed Sulzer, with Sherwin Bash, who also looked after Alpert's group The Tijuana Brass.

Alpert then sent the duo back into the studio to record their second single. Three songs were tried – 'Love is Surrender', 'Help' and 'I'll Never Fall in Love Again' – all of which appeared on the next album, but none of which would be singles. Around this time, Burt Bacharach – the composer of 'I'll Never Fall in Love Again' – saw the duo performing his song live at a benefit event and had been impressed. He invited them to open for him at another benefit concert, and suggested they perform a medley of his music. Richard was flattered, and carefully collated eight songs – 'Any Day Now', 'Baby It's You', 'Knowing When to Leave', 'Make It Easy on Yourself', 'There's Always Something There to Remind Me', 'I'll Never Fall in Love Again', 'Walk On By' and 'Do You Know the Way to San Jose'. An abridged studio recording of this medley was included on the Carpenters' 1971 (Tan) album, and a live recording of the full version as performed in 1974 at Las Vegas' Riviera Hotel appeared on the 1989 Japan compilation *Anthology*.

Whilst Richard was working on his arrangement, Herb Alpert delivered the sheet music for another Bacharach tune: 'They Long to Be Close To You'. Neither of the siblings were familiar with the song, nor particularly cared for it. Since it also didn't fit well with the medley they were rehearsing, the sheet music was left ignored on the piano. Alpert had previously recorded a version of his own with the Tijuana Brass, but feeling that the duo could do it better justice, he insisted they try it out in the studio. It took three attempts and the replacement of Karen's drums by Wrecking Crew drummer Hal Blaine before they reached the definitive recording.

23

The single was scheduled for release in May 1970, backed with 'I Kept on Loving You', but Richard was undecided as to which track would make the stronger A-side. The decision became harder still when he heard a song in a TV advert late one evening and thought he'd discovered an even better choice for their next single. The song was 'We've Only Just Begun', and Richard instantly knew who'd written it, recognising the distinctive vocal of staff A&M writer Paul Williams. Richard found Williams the next day, and asked if there was a full song to accompany the one minute of music he'd heard in the advert. Williams confirmed there was, and the Carpenters soon set about working on their own version, Richard feeling sure it would be a hit.

In the event, '(They Long To Be) Close To You' was released first, entering the *Billboard* Hot 100 at 56 on 17 June 1970. While the single steadily climbed the chart, the band divided their time between TV promotion and recording of their second album.

They also managed to fit in tour dates across the country, many of which were opening for Burt Bacharach. The live band consisted of Danny Woodhams on bass, Bob Messenger on bass, saxophone and flute, Gary Sims on guitar and Doug Strawn on electric clarinet and other woodwinds. While Richard still sang one or two songs, Karen was to emerge as the group's lead vocalist from this point onwards. The band underwent painstaking rehearsals in order to accurately learn every harmony and detail of Richard's arrangements. With the exception of Gary Sims, this live band can be seen in the promotional clip for 'Close To You'. It was filmed in A&M Studio B, where the album was recorded. In the film clip, Richard mimes his acoustic piano part on a Wurlitzer 200A electric piano, while Karen does the same to Hal Blaine's drums, and Woodhams mimes the trumpet part.

Their combined promotional efforts paid off, and the single hit number one in the US on 22 June 1970, achieving gold status and kick-starting a period of phenomenal success for the group. The accompanying *Close To You* album followed in August and rose to number two by December.

Up to this point, the A&M staff had mostly dismissed the group as lightweight, but having a number-one single earned them more respect, especially as the label hadn't had a number-one record for over a year. Clearly, the marketing department still lacked a clear idea of how to promote the duo, when you consider the regrettable cover photo they chose of the pair looking like awkward newlyweds sitting on a grey rocky beach with their hair flattened by sea spray. Nevertheless, the album sold 5,000,000 copies in its first run, peaking at number 2 and going multi-platinum. It also brought them eight Grammy nominations, of which they won Best New Artist and Best Contemporary Vocal Performance by a Group for the single 'Close To You'.

As a result of their success, *Offering* was re-released in November 1970, retitled to *Ticket To Ride*. It was given a new cover photo, taken on a boat on

Lake Tahoe, where the band were playing a residency. Peaking at 150 on the *Billboard* 200, it reached the Top 20 in the UK, Australia and Zimbabwe over the next few years.

'We've Only Just Begun' (Paul Williams, Roger Nichols)
Single A-side b/w 'All of My Life'
Release date: 21 August 1970
Charts: US: 2, UK: 28

According to Richard, their second hit single became the song most associated with the duo. Referring to it in the *From the Top* booklet as their *de facto* 'signature' tune, the song eventually became exactly that on their late-1970s TV specials, albeit in a disco-fied version.

'We've Only Just Begun' was originally written for a Crocker Bank TV commercial. The commission was first assigned to jingle writer Tony Asher, who'd written lyrics for the Beach Boys and Roger Nichols. When Asher broke his arm in a skiing accident, he passed the job to Nichols and his partner Paul Williams. Working to footage of a church wedding, the songwriters created a song that voiced the inner hopes, plans and dreams of a newly married couple. They added the bridge section a short time later, but the whole song was complete by the time Richard became interested. Around the time the Carpenters were working on their recording of it, two other versions were released, though neither Freddie Allen nor Mark Lindsay of Paul Revere and the Raiders succeeded in having hits with the song. The Carpenters' single was released in September 1970, and by October, it reached number two on the *Billboard* Hot 100, held off the number one spot by the Jackson 5's 'I'll Be There', and then by The Partridge Family's 'I Think I Love You'.

The Carpenters' arrangement begins with gentle piano and woodwind. In the original mix, both instruments sound rather distant, which was partly due to being panned to opposite sides of the stereo spectrum. Richard adjusted this in the 1985 and 1991 remixes, giving the parts a more even spread.

Karen delivers the verses softly, before bringing extra power to the bridge sections. In a display of incredible breath control, she sang the whole opening line in one single breath, Richard later noting that most singers insert a breath after the word 'begun'. As the second verse begins with a drum fill, the backing vocals generate a rich, four-part A9 chord, with the outer notes spaced six notes apart. This kind of voicing was to become a signature Carpenters' harmony sound.

Verse two flows smoothly on a pad of strings, and funky bass courtesy of Joe Osborn. By the verse's end, the couple in the lyric have learnt 'to run', indicated by punchy horn blasts and accelerating chord changes. The bridge takes us on a new journey, changing key twice before returning to the verse and the original key of A major. A sudden change to C# major at the very end suggests a bright future for the song's young couple.

'Love Is Surrender' (Ralph Carmichael)

This infectious and upbeat number was adapted from a contemporary Christian song recorded in 1969 by Ralph Carmichael and the Young People. Carmichael – a TV composer and arranger for Nat King Cole – was also a figure in the 1960s Jesus People movement, working on a blend of jazz and pop with Christian hymns to attract younger converts. With Carmichael's permission, the original Christian references were secularised for the Carpenters' recording, wherein lines like 'Without Him, love is not to be found' became 'Without love, you are not to be found'.

In the Carpenters' version, Carmichael's structure is retained, though the tempo is increased, and a new Latin rhythm adopted, complete with Perez Prado-style grunts. Karen sings the opening verse, and Richard sings the second, perhaps to better deliver the line 'You can shout we're all brothers'. A promotional film clip was shot at A&M Studio B in a setup identical to the shoot for 'Close To You', with Karen singing and playing the drums.

The track was remixed in 1987 for inclusion on subsequent compilations, with new reverb and new bass and kick-drum parts.

'Maybe It's You' (Richard Carpenter, John Bettis)

Written in 1968 for Spectrum, this song was revived for the second album. Karen describes a romantic walk along the beach with an idealised partner – 'the Ocean King' – whose 'only thought is love for me'. Yet, as perfect as things may seem, the narrator is still unsure of the relationship – 'Maybe it's wise, maybe it's not' – the song ending on an ambiguous chord.

The recording is a good example of how clearly and carefully Karen enunciated words, possibly as a result of her choir training. She also seems to be adopting a British or mid-Atlantic accent, and Richard has commented on how she was influenced by British singer Matt Monro, a favourite singer of their mother, Agnes.

During sessions for the album, two takes were recorded of the line 'Never been the kind who can pass a lucky penny by'. The second one was used, though there was some concern that it didn't quite fit with the other vocals' tonal qualities. In 1987, Richard replaced his acoustic piano with a Yamaha DX-7 electric piano part, but the 'lucky penny' line remained unchanged, and this version made it onto two compilations. For the 1990 remix, the original acoustic piano was restored, and the first originally unused take of the 'lucky penny' line was used, as heard on subsequent compilations.

'Reason To Believe' (Tim Hardin)

Folk singer Tim Hardin – composer of the popular '60s hit 'If I Were a Carpenter' – released the equally popular 'Reason to Believe' on his 1966 debut album. Many covers followed, including those by Peter, Paul and Mary, Marianne Faithfull and Glen Campbell, though the best-known is arguably Rod Stewart's 1971 version.

In the lyric, the narrator struggles to find forgiveness for a lover who is both desirable and deceitful. In the Carpenters' version, the chorus harmonies sound so sympathetic that we can be sure the errant lover has gotten away with their deception once again.

The chorus is only heard once in Hardin's original, but other versions repeat it, as the Carpenters do here. Strings add a sophisticated *countrypolitan* air, Wurlitzer electric piano and guitar add rolling patterns and country licks, while Karen keeps it all moving with a country rhythm. As their first country recording, the duo revisited the genre throughout their career, just as their mentors, The Beatles, had done. Speaking of whom ...

'Help' (John Lennon, Paul McCartney)

From the moment of its release in 1965, this Beatles classic attracted a range of interpretations, from gospel singer Clara Ward to comedian Peter Sellers, and from avant-garde opera singer Cathy Berberian to rock band Deep Purple. The Carpenters reimagine the song with added harmonies, keyboards in place of guitars, and soulful trumpets in the style of the group Chicago.

Where The Beatles launch their version with a startling one-time introductory section, the Carpenters' version goes straight to the opening verse lines. Richard plays a church-like Hammond organ part that lends an air of gospel testimony to Karen's vocal. She also adds soprano parts to the backing choir. The overall effect is highly dramatic, and it is clear why they used the song as an attention-grabbing opening number in their early shows. They even considered releasing it as their second single, to follow 'Ticket To Ride'. The exclamation mark that's part of The Beatles' song title – 'Help!' – was left off by mistake.

Richard and Karen were delighted to learn that their admiration for The Beatles was reciprocated. While touring the UK in 1973, they spent an evening with Paul McCartney at 10cc's Strawberry Studios in Stockport near Manchester, where McCartney was recording an album with his brother Mike McGear. According to songwriter and producer Nicky Chinn (as quoted in Coleman's biography), Karen encountered John Lennon at a Los Angeles restaurant, where he reportedly said, 'I just want to tell you, love, that I think you've got a fabulous voice'.

'(They Long To Be) Close To You' (Burt Bacharach, Hal David)
Single A-side b/w 'I Kept on Loving You'
Release date: 15 May 1970
Charts: US: 1, UK: 6

Side one closes with their first number-one single and the first of three Burt Bacharach songs. Bacharach and his lyricist Hal David wrote the song in the early 1960s, and the first recording was by actor Richard Chamberlain. Dionne Warwick and Dusty Springfield also released it, but no one had yet had a hit with it when Herb Alpert brought it to the Carpenters. He wanted them to approach it with fresh ears and asked them to avoid listening to previous versions. While neither Richard nor Karen were especially enthusiastic about the song, they proceeded anyway at Alpert's urging.

Once they were in the studio, it took several attempts to arrive at a recording that pleased everyone. Alpert rejected the first attempt, feeling Karen was taking the wrong approach, singing with an overly casual air that was too close to Harry Nilsson's singing style. Alpert also wanted session players on piano and drums. Pianist Larry Knechtel and drummer Hal Blaine were hired – two established Wrecking Crew musicians who'd recently played on Simon and Garfunkel's 'Bridge Over Troubled Water'. Both had played together on many hits with Joe Osborn, and they were known collectively as the Hollywood Golden Trio.

When Knechtel's piano style was considered too strident for 'Close To You', Richard returned to the keys. Also, Blaine's drumming style was much heavier than Karen's, but Alpert felt this provided the power that the song had previously lacked. By Richard's estimate, it took over 40 takes to get the ideal backing track. Blaine attributes this to the band getting faster, as, to his ear, the introduction, middle and ending were all played at different speeds. To remedy this, he recommended they play to a metronome click track. Richard initially objected, being a musician who preferred to play by feel. However, when he noticed the significant improvement the click track brought, he resolved to use it on future sessions.

Richard modified Bacharach's song by adding the now-familiar piano introduction, which is doubled by vibraphone chimes that float in the gap between the intro and Karen's first words. Her delivery is intimate and sincere, and mouth-movement sounds are audible, revealing just how close she was to the microphone. While earlier versions of the song kept to a straight rhythm, Richard's arrangement is a shuffle with a gentle swing, and Karen emphasises that rhythm with an extra syllable to the word 'C-lose' in the choruses. A harp glissando leads to the middle section, where angels 'sprinkle moondust in your hair', illustrated by Richard playing two descending quintuplet piano patterns. When Bacharach granted permission for the duo to record the song, he insisted on this particular detail of the piano part being retained.

Backing vocals are saved until the third verse, arranged – as ever – in inverted chords with outer notes an interval of a 6th apart. The key shifts up a semitone for the flugelhorn solo, played by Chuck Findley in a style closely resembling that of Herb Alpert. The flugelhorn part was thickened by recording it four times. Another burst of harp leads into the solo's second half, where Richard plays a harmonised version of the melody.

For the ending, Richard reprised the piano intro. Sensing that more was needed to guarantee a hit, he conceived the memorable 'waah' outro, written as a tribute to the entirely new piece of music heard at the end of Bacharach's 'Raindrops Keep Falling On My Head'. To sing the 'waah' vocal part, the duo layered their voices 12 times, taking advantage of A&M's recent conversion to 16-track recording. While the single fades at 3:40, the album version has an extended outro, growing out of two octave piano notes that Richard improvised along to the click track 'for fun', according to the band's website. Hal Blaine then plays a tom fill, and the band return to the coda section.

When Alpert asked Richard how well he thought the song would do in the charts, Schmidt's biography reports that Richard replied it would either be number one or a 'monumental stiff. No in-between'. Happily, it was a monumental hit, holding the number one spot for four weeks during its 17-week US chart stay. The single went gold and earned the duo their first Grammy award, presented the following year. Alpert's instinct had proven to be correct, as the song took off in a further 14 countries. Over 400 covers have been recorded since, including a recent Frank Ocean interpretation, and those by UK singer Rumer and the cast of *Glee*. Translations have been done in at least 13 languages, including Czech, Danish and Hebrew.

'Baby It's You' (Burt Bacharach, Mack David, Barney Williams)
This song by Bacharach and Hal David's brother Mack David was originally titled 'I'll Cherish You', until Shirelles producer Luther Dixon changed the lyric to have the narrator defending their unfaithful boyfriend. Dixon was credited under the pseudonym Barney Williams. Following The Shirelles' earlier success with 'Will You Still Love Me Tomorrow?', in 1961, they had a hit with 'Baby It's You'. The Beatles covered the song on their first album, *Please Please Me*, in 1963.

The Carpenters' version was slower, and the 'sha la la' backing vocals were saved for the outro. Beginning with piano accompaniment, the drama builds throughout as Karen lays down a discreetly funky drum rhythm, and Bob Messenger plays slinky saxophone lines. Karen's vocal builds in a similar way, rising from intimate to intense by the second chorus.

In later years, Karen complained that Richard often didn't tell her what song was being recorded until they arrived at the studio. In this instance, she was clearly familiar with the song, repeating words, adding melismatic phrases and generally making it her own.

'I'll Never Fall In Love Again' (Burt Bacharach, Hal David)
The Bacharach trilogy concludes with a song written for the successful 1968 Broadway musical *Promises Promises,* which was based on Billy Wilder's 1960 film *The Apartment*. Onstage, the number was a veritable showstopper, the droll lyric rhyming 'pneumonia' with 'he'll never phone ya'. Dionne Warwick and Bobby Gentry took their versions into the charts in the late-1960s.

Karen varies her vocal approach as if trying on different personas, sounding vampish in the bridge section, petulant on 'those chains', and growling the phrase 'that is why...'. She also provides the unearthly theremin-like portamento sweep on the 'here to remind you' backing vocal at 1:56, reaching a high F note. When the music returns, Richard's keyboard part appears to be quoting from the Bacharach song 'This Guy's in Love With You', which could've been a nod to A&M label boss Herb Alpert, who'd taken the song to number 1 in 1968.

'Crescent Noon' (Richard Carpenter, John Bettis)

Another early Carpenter/Bettis composition, this slow and chilly lament was directly influenced by the first piece from Eric Satie's famous 1888 piano work 'Trois Gymnopédies'. It's interesting to note that in 1968, American group Blood, Sweat and Tears opened their eponymous second album with a variation on Satie's composition, which might have been an influence on Carpenter and Bettis.

The poetic lyric of 'Crescent Noon' contains colourful pastoral descriptions such as 'October brown' and 'midnight blue' – personifying nature with clouds that cry, mountains that are born, and seasons that stumble into each other. Karen holds long notes throughout the mournful minor-key verses, though the mood is brightened each time the major-key chorus arrives. Karen and Richard form a choir for the third verse, before chilly strings and woodwind blasts lead to Karen's secluded solo voice in the final verse.

A recording from 1969 exists of Karen and Richard performing the song with the CSULB choir. Though unreleased, it can be found online.

'Mr Guder' (Richard Carpenter, John Bettis)

Another early song from late 1967, this was written as a pithy riposte to one Victor Guder – the manager who hired and fired Carpenter and Bettis from their summer positions at Disneyland in summer 1967. The pair had worked as turn-of-the-century musicians at the Coke Corner café on Main Street, U.S.A, with Richard on piano and Bettis on banjo. Dressed smartly in straw boaters, waistcoats and black ties, their directive was to play songs from the vaudeville era. However, they were also happy to oblige customer requests for contemporary songs, including The Beatles' 'Yesterday', The Doors' 'Light My Fire', and 'Somewhere, My Love': a recent hit based on 'Lara's Theme' from the film *Doctor Zhivago*. This kind of dissension led to their dismissal, and the pair responded by pouring their frustration into the musical kiss off 'Mr Guder'.

In the lyric, Guder is lampooned for his neat and tidy image and adherence to the company rules, extending the anti-establishment theme of 'Your Wonderful Parade' from the group's first album. The accompaniment mixes Latin rhythm with baroque harpsichord, and fast and slow tempo changes. The instrumental section features Bob Messenger's jazz-like flute solo, eventually building to an *a cappella* vocalese breakdown reminiscent of French vocal group The Swingle Singers. In the end, Guder is urged to 'Play your game, stay the same', and the gentle outro appears to lull him back into his somnambulant existence.

The song was part of the band's early sets, though Richard later came to regret the directness of the public slur. Karen's biographer Randy Schmidt tracked down Victor Guder, and thankfully, he appeared to have taken the tongue-lashing in good faith. Bob Messenger re-recorded his flute parts in 1990 when the track was remixed for subsequent compilations.

'I Kept On Loving You' (Paul Williams, Roger Nichols)

This carefree number has Richard's only lead vocal on the album. The narrator pleads for forgiveness in a lyric that could serve as an answer to 'Reason to Believe'. The breezy acoustic guitar, agile electric-guitar fills, soothing flute and snappy trumpet all contribute to the bright, cheerful mood, while the bass adds some cool fills in the closing section.

'Another Song' (Richard Carpenter, John Bettis)

This is reputed to be the first written Carpenter/Bettis song. An early version was recorded by their vocal group Spectrum at United Audio Recording Studios in 1967, though it has never been released.

The song is structured in five different sections, the first lasting only 20 seconds and based on a passage from 'And lo! The Angel of the Lord Came Upon Them': part one of Handel's *Messiah*. In contrast, the second section is in a dramatic rock style, and Karen's vocal changes to desperation as she relates her companion's mysterious departure. The story is extended through two more short sections, the second offering hope of a new start and 'another song to sing', before returning to the earlier dramatic section. The final section is a long psychedelic instrumental sounding vaguely Arabic as a flute plays modal snake-charmer phrases over rolling drums, wah pedal keyboard and free-flowing bass lines. This jam session provides space for each musician to stretch out and flaunt their skills, concluding the album in a burst of energy. Stylistically closer to the sound of The Doors or Jethro Tull, 'Another Song' could've easily been called 'Another Band', since its fusion-rock style is quite unlike any other Carpenters recordings.

Related Tracks
'Get Together'/'Interview' *Your Navy Presents*

In March 1970, at A&M Studio C, the group recorded songs for the Navy's Public Service Program, which was aimed at naval servicemen and was broadcast weekly on 2500 radio stations. The band submitted 14 songs to be included in four shows lasting approximately 15 minutes each. The selections are a fair representation of the band's live set at this time, and include three that were never recorded for albums. 12 of the songs were recorded live at A&M, along with two partially mixed versions of 'Love is Surrender' and 'Help' from *Close To You*. The 12 live recordings were: 'Ticket To Ride', 'Nowadays Clancy Can't Even Sing', 'All I Can Do', 'All of My Life', 'Cinderella Rockerfella', 'Mr Guder', 'I Fell in Love With You', 'Get Together', 'Bacharach/

David Medley', 'Can't Buy Me Love', 'Baby It's You' and 'Flat Baroque'.

'Cinderella Rockerfella' is a frivolous cover of the 1967 novelty hit by Israeli duo Esther and Abi Ofarim, which Karen sings with Doug Strawn. 'I Fell in Love With You' is a hilarious tongue-in-cheek number also sung by Doug and Karen. A version of the song can be heard in the 1971 *Live at the BBC* concert that's currently available online.

The Carpenters' version of The Beatles' 'Can't Buy Me Love' has a soulful, funky rhythm and saxophone breaks. The 'Bacharach/David Medley' follows the same shortened order as on the *Carpenters* (Tan) album. In a change to the version on *Offering/Ticket To Ride*, 'Get Together' features Karen on lead vocal instead of Richard, and the tremolo effect is not used on Karen's vocal. This song – with a scripted and factually inaccurate interview from the program – was included on the compilations *From the Top* and *The Essential Collection: 1965-1997,* while bootleg recordings of the other 13 tracks can currently be found online.

'Merry Christmas, Darling' (Richard Carpenter, Frank Pooler)
Single A-side b/w 'Mr Guder'
Release date: 22 November 1970
Charts: US Holiday 100: 1, UK: 45
This song began as a lyric CSULB choir leader Frank Pooler wrote for his girlfriend in 1946 when he knew they'd be spending Christmas apart. He'd struggled to find the right melody, and had put the song aside. But in 1966, he passed it to Richard to see if he could complete it. Being a fan of Christmas songs, Richard apparently needed only ten minutes to set the words to music. The Carpenters road-tested the song at Christmas performances over the next few years, before finally recording it in November 1970 during the same session as 'For All We Know'. The Christmas song was a hit on *Billboard*'s Holiday 100 chart, reaching number one in 1970, and again in 1971 and 1973.

The song structure resembles a jazz standard, with an opening introductory verse that's heard only once. The arrangement includes a celesta making a tinkling snowfall sound, a classy saxophone solo from Bob Messenger, and a carolling choir whose voices cascade in a canon at the end. Hal Blaine was the drummer. Karen wasn't entirely happy with her vocal, and re-recorded it in 1978 for the *Christmas Portrait* album, though the original vocal can be heard on the compilations *From the Top* and *The Essential Collection: 1965-1997.*

Carpenters (Tan Album) (1971)

Personnel:
Karen Carpenter: vocals, drums
Richard Carpenter: vocals, keyboards, orchestrator, arranger
Joe Osborn: bass
Jim Horn: woodwinds
Doug Strawn: reeds
Bob Messenger: bass, reeds
Tommy Morgan: harmonica (1)
Hal Blaine: drums
Produced by Jack Daugherty
Engineered by Ray Gerhardt, Dick Bogert and Norm Kinney
Recorded at A&M Records, Hollywood, California
Release date: 14 May 1971
Label: A&M
Charts: US: 2 UK: 11
Running Time 31:26

With the breakthrough success of 'Close To You', the Carpenters found themselves in demand throughout 1970 and 1971, embarking on a relentless touring schedule across the States, Canada and Japan. Initial appearances saw them supporting acts like Bread and Engelbert Humperdinck, but the Carpenters soon became headliners, playing Carnegie Hall and what became the biggest date of their career so far at the Ohio State Fair in front of 50,000 people.

They also found time for TV appearances on *The Tonight Show Starring Johnny Carson, The Ed Sullivan Show* and *The Andy Williams Show*. In February 1971, the duo were honoured a little prematurely with their own episode of *This is Your Life* before performing at the Grammy Awards the following month. From July to September 1971, they starred in *Make Your Own Kind of Music*: a weekly variety show named after the hit song by Mama Cass. Miming to tracks from their first three albums, they also performed songs by The Monkees, The Beatles, and Bacharach and David.

With such a busy promotional schedule, there was little time left for studio work. Fortunately, the third album *Carpenters* was one of their strongest, and includes some of their best-known tunes, including 'Rainy Days And Mondays' and 'Superstar'. Recording took place in A&M studios A, B and C, beginning in late 1970 with 'For All We Know', which in January 1971 was the album's first single.

The album reunited Richard and lyricist John Bettis, who'd walked out two years earlier after a disagreement. Richard also worked with Ron Gorow, who orchestrated Richard's ideas. Karen is the main drummer, and Hal Blaine was hired for the singles, suggesting that they had already decided on the singles in advance.

The album cover featured the new Carpenters logo created by designer Craig Braun and illustrator Walter Velez. The sleeve folded out to make a standing picture frame showing a portrait of Karen and Richard. The cover's resemblance to a brown envelope earned *Carpenters* the nickname *The Tan Album*, in the same way, The Beatles' eponymous 1968 album was unofficially rechristened *The White Album*.

With over 1,000,000 pre-orders, the record shipped gold and eventually went four times platinum, becoming the duo's best-selling album. It remained in the *Billboard* Hot 100 albums for over a year, spending six months in the top 10. All three singles reached the top 3 and went gold. The album was nominated for three Grammys, winning Best Pop Vocal Performance by a Group. The *Billboard* magazine review praised Karen's 'sparkling voice' and Richard's 'sophisticated, contemporary arrangements'. The album remains the favourite for many fans.

'Rainy Days And Mondays' (Paul Williams, Roger Nichols)
Single A-side b/w 'Saturday'
Release date: 23 April 1971
Charts: US: 2, UK: 53
While the Carpenters were the first to release this melancholy song, Williams and Nichols had written it for The 5th Dimension, who turned it down. The song intended instead for the Carpenters was Paul Williams' 'An Old Fashioned Love Song', which Richard wasn't keen on, leaving the way clear for Three Dog Night to take it to number four in October 1971.

'Rainy Days And Mondays' begins with Tommy Morgan's harmonica, matching the lyric's 'blues' reference, and providing a second voice to complement Karen's. The opening line, 'Talking to myself and feeling old', came from Paul Williams' observation of how his mother often talked to herself. Karen was just turning 21 when she sang about feeling old, though her voice conveys a much greater maturity – beginning the song on a low G as if to convey age and experience. Following Bob Messenger's smooth saxophone solo and a repeat of the bridge, the key moves up a tone and Karen sings the final chorus powerfully, holding her last note for three bars.

A promotional film clip was shot at the Desert Inn, Las Vegas. The single reached number 2 in June 1971, kept from number 1 by Carole King's double A-side 'It's Too Late'/'I Feel the Earth Move'.'Rainy Days And Mondays' was remixed in 1985 for the *Yesterday Once More* compilation, and again in 1991 with enhanced bass and with the strings removed from behind the sax solo: as found on the *Gold* and *Singles 1969 to 1981* collections.

'Saturday' (Richard Carpenter, John Bettis)
From maudlin Mondays to ever-lovin' Saturdays and the first of the album's three Richard lead vocals. At 1:18 in length, this light and breezy number is something of a palate cleanser between two compelling Williams/Nichols

ballads. Perky Tijuana Brass-style trumpets play descending patterns in 3/4 time before the verse settles into a regular 4/4 meter. The giddy lyric is filled with 'bluebirds', 'flowers' and 'laughter', and Karen's brushes help the song skip along. Following a brief trumpet solo, the key changes up a half step.

Written for Spectrum back in 1967, 'Saturday' belongs in a special category of 1960s songs that celebrate weekends, including The Easybeats' 'Friday on My Mind' and 'Groovin'' by The Young Rascals.

'Let Me Be The One' (Paul Williams, Roger Nichols)
Following the final beat of 'Saturday', this is the second of two Williams/Nichols ballads and has also been recorded by Jack Jones, Anne Murray, Petula Clark and others.

The subdued four-bar verses are short but memorable. Karen's vocal is doubled on the choruses. In the *From the Top* booklet, Richard remarked on the 'intimate reading' that Karen gave the bridge, which closes with a bar in 3/4 time. The outro is filled with inventive bass runs and drum fills that Richard specifically notated for Joe Osborn and Hal Blaine.

The duo felt the track could've been a single, but 'Superstar' was issued instead. In 1991, a remix was issued as a promotional single to launch the *From the Top* collection. That version incorporates Karen's vocal warm-ups, the original studio count-in, and the full ending rather than the original fade-out.

'(A Place To) Hide Away' (Randy Sparks)
This gentle ballad's writer, Randy Sparks, is best known as the founder of The New Christy Minstrels – an early-1960s folk group that helped launch the careers of Barry McGuire (who sang lead on their hits 'Green, Green' and 'Three Wheels On My Wagon'), Gene Clark of The Byrds, Kenny Rogers and Kim Carnes. Richard and Karen first heard Sparks performing '(A Place to) Hide Away' in 1967 when Spectrum were booked to play at his West Los Angeles club Ledbetter's. In an interview on the website *Carpenters Avenue*, Sparks states how he'd lost confidence in this song soon after he wrote it, only performing it once at Ledbetter's. He was, therefore, very surprised to learn that the Carpenters had remembered it and recorded a version four years later.

That story doesn't explain the existence of a 1967 recording of the song by the Detroit duo Gaylord and Holiday. Their version can be found online, and their arrangement is in 6/8 time. Richard's arrangement is in 4/4 time and embellished with some unexpected chord sequences in the intro and outro.

'For All We Know' (Fred Karlin, Arthur James, Robb Wilson)
Single A-side b/w 'Don't Be Afraid'
Release date: 15 January 1971
Charts: US: 3, UK: 18

While 'We've Only Just Begun' was making headway in the charts, A&M urged the duo to record a follow-up, as the label was unwilling to release further singles from *Close To You*. Looking for material, the ideal candidate presented itself in October 1970 when the duo took a night off on their first Canadian tour, to go to the cinema. Their manager Sherwin Bash had recommended they see the romantic comedy *Lovers and Other Strangers*, which follows a young couple as they prepare for their wedding. The film's main love theme, 'For All We Know' (sung on the soundtrack by Larry Meredith), immediately caught Richard's attention, and he made arrangements for the publisher's demo recording and lead sheet to be waiting for him as soon as they returned from the tour.

The music was written by film composer Fred Karlin, while the lyricists Arthur James and Robb Wilson were actually pen names for Jimmy Griffin and Robb Royer from the band Bread.

The Larry Meredith recording begins with acoustic guitar, and the Carpenters were planning to begin their version in a similar way following a chance meeting with guitarist/singer José Feliciano at an L.A. restaurant. When recording began in December 1970, Feliciano came to the studio and played the opening melody. Unfortunately, an angry phone call came from Feliciano's manager, and the part had to be removed. Oboe player Jim Horn then came in to play the melody. (This oboe part was replaced by Earle Dumler in the 1990 remix.)

Karen's vocal tone sounds rich and pure, and she begins on a low G before the verse melody climbs up an octave to a high A on 'so much to say'.

The backing vocals create a four-note chord on the syllable 'Waah' towards the end of the song. Subsequent remixes add extra reverb and enhance Karen's voice and the bass.

The single reached three on the *Billboard* charts, achieving gold status and auguring well for the forthcoming album.

'Superstar' (Leon Russell, Bonnie Bramlett)
Single A-side b/w 'Bless the Beasts and the Children'
Release date: 12 August 1971
Charts: US: 2
Double A-side single b/w 'For All We Know' (UK release)
Release date: 3 September 1971
Charts: UK: 18

Side two starts with one of the duo's most popular recordings, having inspired over 140 cover versions, including those by Roberta Flack, Elkie Brooks, Belinda Carlisle and Luther Vandross.

In a BBC Radio 2 documentary, songwriter Leon Russell recalled that the idea for the song came from hearing Rita Coolidge describing singer Dionne Warwick as a 'superstar'. Intrigued by what was then a new term, he began the song, and singer Bonnie Bramlett helped him finish it. Some sources also credit Bramlett's husband, Delaney, as a contributor.

The working title was 'Groupie Song', becoming 'Groupie (Superstar)' for its first release as the B-side to the minor 1969 hit 'Comin' Home' by Delaney & Bonnie and Friends featuring Eric Clapton. The title evolved to 'Superstar' when Cher released a non-charting version in 1970. That year, Rita Coolidge performed the song as part of Joe Cocker's *Mad Dogs and Englishmen* tour; A&M Records coincidentally sponsored the tour and released the live album.

Richard first encountered the song in January 1971 when Bette Midler performed it on Johnny Carson's *Tonight Show*. But Richard had to ask around as to what the song title was since it wasn't stated in the lyric. He then realised he already owned an unplayed copy of *Mad Dogs and Englishmen* that he'd picked up at A&M. One of the first changes he made was to the line 'I can hardly wait to sleep with you again', opting for the less-explicit phrase 'to be with you again', bearing in mind the importance of radio-play and the band's mainstream appeal. He also adjusted the arrangement, steering away from the theatrics of Midler's version, as arranged by her musical director, Barry Manilow. Richard's interpretation was more subtle, with an ominous low piano note struck in the middle of each verse, and the descending French horn chords that lead from the introduction into the first verse. Richard expanded these horn parts when remixing the track for the 1985 *Yesterday Once More* collection, playing additional notes on a Kurzweil synthesizer.

Despite the reference to guitar in the lyric, Richard resisted adding one to the arrangement, which is fitting since the guitarist is absent from the young woman's life. However, a guitar *does* appear on the 2018 re-recording with the Royal Philharmonic Orchestra.

Karen's emotive reading is truly captivating as she sings the opening lines in a single breath, drawing the words out with sustain and vibrato. Despite the performance's strong conviction, Karen apparently had little enthusiasm for the song until she came to hear the final playback. According to Randy Schmidt's Karen biography, the vocal take used was just a guide intended to be replaced later. Schmidt also notes that Karen sang the lyric off a paper napkin hastily written out by Richard in the studio.

The band filmed a promo clip on the stage at the Desert Inn, Las Vegas. Though they were appearing at the Sands at the time, the Desert Inn was chosen for its larger stage. The single was the final from the album and became a sizable hit, reaching 2 in *Billboard* in October 1971. It was kept from the top spot by Rod Stewart's 'Maggie May' (b/w his version of 'Reason to Believe').

Around this time, Bette Midler was cracking jokes at Karen's expense in her live act, attacking the singer's clean-cut image and deriding her drumming skills. In a twist of fate, Midler won the 1974 Grammy for Best New Artist, and her statue was presented to her by Karen and Richard, former winners of the same award. Acknowledging the moment's awkwardness, Midler sheepishly told the audience, 'I'm surprised she didn't hit me over the head with it', before swiftly exiting the stage.

'Druscilla Penny' (Richard Carpenter, John Bettis)

Sticking with the theme of groupies, 'Druscilla Penny' is more satire than tragedy. The disdainful lyric – delivered by Richard – pokes fun at the paraphernalia and affectations of the young girls who chased after rock bands. Seizing on the spirit of the times, the character's outlandish name recalls the names of real-life groupies such as Cynthia Plaster Caster or Suzy Creamcheese.

The key musical ingredient for this Restoration-style comedy of morals is a harpsichord played in the Baroque style of pieces by JS Bach or Vivaldi. The instrument also became associated with 1960s psychedelia via recordings like The Yardbirds' 'For Your Love' and The Beatles' 'Fixing a Hole'.

Tension rises throughout the verse as the chords step up chromatically via diminished voicings before the eventual tension release with the final major chord. The bridge section is reminiscent of cycle-of-fourths progressions heard in baroque music, such as the 'VI: Passacaglia' section from George Frideric Handel's 'Suite No. 7 in G minor'.

The comedy is carried over into the backing vocals, where the girl's mother cries for her daughter. At the end, an *a cappella* choir repeats Richard's final 'No!' in the manner of a religious antiphonal response.

The caustic lyric was originally written to settle a score between Richard and a police officer who'd held him in jail overnight for a minor traffic violation after a gig in Miami. That lyric gave the officer's real name and was rejected by manager Sherwin Bash. Richard and Bettis then rewrote the lyric to be about a fictitious groupie, though the name Druscilla Penny was the pseudonym of an actual woman that Bettis knew. Needless to say, that Druscilla didn't consider the song to be a compliment.

'One Love' (Richard Carpenter, John Bettis)

In 1967, when Richard and Bettis worked at Disneyland, they both fell in love with a waitress named Candy. Composing a song named after her, the lyric was subsequently revised into a general ode to romance for the Carpenters' third album.

Woodwinds, strings and harp all contribute to the romantic mood, while Karen sings with a sense of longing. The bass guitar descends chromatically through the verse, settling on a pedal note that underpins the hymn-like bridge. For that section, the key changes to the major 6th, and the duo create a chamber choir, issuing cautionary advice. The song ends on an optimistic thought, with Karen sustaining her final note across two bars.

'Bacharach/David Medley' (Burt Bacharach, Hal David)

In 1970, the Carpenters performed a 15-minute medley of eight Bacharach/David songs when appearing as Bacharach's opening act. In this studio version, 'Any Day Now' and 'Baby It's You' are dropped, leaving six songs. Richard has explained that the medley was played too fast – a habit the band adopted performing the song on TV when producers had asked them to make it shorter. Short of new album material, and pushed for time themselves, the medley was chosen to fill space, captured in one live take by the well-honed touring lineup.

The medley begins with 'Knowing When to Leave' from the 1968 musical *Promises, Promises*. The Carpenters' version borrows its introduction from Dionne Warwick's 1970 recording, adding a Latin rhythm. Karen delivers the lyric so rapidly that the song is brought to a conclusion in just 90 seconds.

The pace slows for a chorus of the 1962 song 'Make It Easy on Yourself': the oldest song in the selection. It was already well-known from recordings by Dionne Warwick and The Walker Brothers, and this familiarity allowed the Carpenters to take some liberties, stretching the word 'self' over two syllables and pausing the music for a cascading canon of voices.

The tempo picks up again with 'There's Always Something There to Remind Me', which was a UK number 1 for Sandie Shaw in 1964. Karen leads the lush harmony arrangement, while Latin rhythms and vocal whoops provide a foundation for Richard's busy Wurlitzer solo, throughout most of which the bass guitar keeps to the same one note.

Next comes 'I'll Never Fall in Love Again', as heard in a version on the *Close To You* album. Richard then takes over lead vocals for 'Walk On By': a top-10 hit for Dionne Warwick in 1964. Karen plays an energetic Latin rhythm, adding drum fills and taking over the vocals on the choruses. The medley concludes with 'Do You Know the Way to San José?': a top-10 hit for Dionne Warwick in 1968. The Carpenters' version features close-harmony backing vocals that rise and fall chromatically on the ending 'woah woah' phrases.

'Sometimes' (Henry Mancini, Felice Mancini)
After the prior track's frantic energy, the album closes with a light ballad. Henry Mancini wrote this song after receiving a Christmas card from his daughter Felice. He was so touched by the message, that he set her words to music and took the song directly to Richard and Karen. They decided to record a piano/vocal presentation like Mancini's demo, and it's their only studio recording to apply such a simple setting.

Related Tracks
'And When He Smiles' (Alan Anderson)
This is available on the compilation *As Time Goes By*, and was recorded in September 1971 for the BBC concert that aired in the UK two months later. The track has not appeared on any other Carpenters album.

Originally titled 'And When She Smiles', the song was first recorded in 1970 by Wildweeds – a Connecticut band whose frontman Al Anderson later joined the eclectic rock band NRBQ. (In 1977, the Carpenters were to record 'You're the One' by NRBQ member Steve Ferguson.)

Apart from the title gender change, the Carpenters' version stays fairly close to the original, but with a few additions, such as Bob Messenger's flute part, Doug Strawn's clarinet, Jim Squeglia (billed as Jim Anthony) on bongos, and a Latin rhythm in the middle section.

A Song For You (1972)

Personnel:
Karen Carpenter: vocals, drums
Richard Carpenter: vocals, keyboards, orchestrator, arranger
Joe Osborn: bass
Tony Peluso, Louie Shelton: guitar
Red Rhodes: steel guitar
Bob Messenger: flute, alto flute, tenor saxophone
Earle Dumler: oboe, English horn
Norm Herzberg: bassoon
Tim Weisberg: bass flute (4)
Gary Coleman: percussion (3)
Hal Blaine: drums
Special thanks to Ron Gorow
Produced by Jack Daugherty
Engineered by Ray Gerhardt and Roger Young
Recorded at A&M Records, Hollywood, California
Release date: 13 June 1972
Label: A&M
Charts: US: 4, UK: 13 (1973)
Running Time 36:57

Carpenters and *A Song For You* were issued just over a year apart, and the interim months were filled with single releases, TV appearances and a busy schedule of live concerts. Though the focus was mainly on touring the States, in September 1971, they made their first trip to the UK, to perform at London's Royal Albert Hall. From there, they headed north to Manchester to record a BBC TV special, combining live and lip-synched performances. While in Europe, they filmed further French and German TV appearances before playing a concert in Bussum, Netherlands. They then resumed touring the States until the end of November. Picking up again in January, their 1972 US dates kept them on the road for most of the year, with trips to Australia, Hong Kong and Japan in May and June.

Concert dates also meant reviews, and critics were noticing that the shows lacked a central focus. They complained that Karen was barely visible when singing from behind her drum kit, and with Richard also seated at the piano, audiences were left unsure of where to look. Some even saw Karen's drumming as a gimmick, since female drummers were still a rarity at the time. Karen's predecessors were few, save for jazz drummers like Viola Smith, Dottie Dodgion, and a small number of contemporaries like Moe Tucker of The Velvet Underground and Alice de Buhr of Fanny.

Despite the increase in lead vocals, Karen was still happiest behind the drums and had recently taken delivery of a unique custom-designed kit. Inspired by Hal Blaine's setup, the new kit included a freestanding rack of four toms, though these only served to hide Karen from the audience even further.

As their fame grew, TV producers, band management and Richard all pressured Karen to come out from behind the kit and stand at the front. With huge reluctance, she eventually agreed to a compromise – playing drums on the faster numbers, and stepping into the spotlight to sing the ballads. Similarly, in the studio, Karen's role as drummer was to decrease over time. Old Connecticut school friend Jim Squeglia was hired as the second drummer for the concerts, going by the stage name Jim Anthony.

Self-conscious and shy, Karen admitted to feeling petrified in her new role as lead singer, often appearing uncertain of her movements at the microphone. Worse still, reviewers now shifted their focus to her clothes and body shape, which undoubtedly contributed to the excessive dieting that led to Karen's untimely death.

Karen and Richard were known to place high demands on themselves and each other, quarrelling in their pursuit of perfection. Band members received dirty looks onstage and tongue-lashings after the show if they dared improvise or deviate from Richard's arrangements. All the same, the musicians' loyalty and commitment were self-evident, with many serving as group members throughout the duo's career. The bigger problem for Richard was the amount of time spent promoting the band on the road when their albums were clearly selling extremely well by themselves. It later became clear to Richard how the vested interests of their management and booking agency were keeping the band on tour when they could've spent more time in the studio perfecting their albums.

Despite their busy schedule, they managed to fit sessions in at A&M from December 1971 to March 1972, recording what many consider to be their best album, *A Song For You*. Nine of the 13 tracks became either single A or B sides, with a tenth – 'Piano Picker' – becoming a popular mainstay of their live set. As before, the band demonstrated their musical range, alternating dramatic ballads with lighter numbers. Engineer Roger Young joined the team at this point, staying for all their future albums, including Richard's solo releases and 1980s and 1990s remixes.

Though the album *does* contain some of their best-known love songs, Richard was dismayed when A&M packaged it like a Valentine's Day card, with a deep red background and an ivory heart. Luckily, the music would win out over the schmaltzy cover, and the album sold millions, going three times platinum and spending 30 weeks on the *Billboard* Hot 100. In 1972, the Carpenters were undeniably on top of the world.

'A Song For You' (Leon Russell)

Having covered Leon Russell's 'Superstar', the duo chose another of his mesmerising songs to open the album. First released on Russell's eponymous 1970 debut album, the haunting melody and direct lyric attracted covers from the likes of Helen Reddy, Jack Jones, and Donny Hathaway, whose version later inspired Amy Winehouse to record her own. Richard first heard the song from the 1971 single by singer, actress and TV panellist Jaye P. Morgan.

Bypassing the original's tumbling piano introduction, the Carpenters' version begins with Karen's intimately delivered opening verse. The arrangement ebbs and flows, featuring a bewitching choral moment just after the bridge. Bob Messenger's sublime saxophone solo was improvised across four takes, with Richard selecting his favourite lines to assemble the solo.

Throughout the album's recording, Karen was beset with sores on her vocal cords, and her doctor told her to take a month's rest. Committed to completing the record, she took two days rest before returning to the studio, though the throat condition was affecting her ability to pitch correctly. In Lennox and May's book *Carpenters: The Musical Legacy*, Richard commented that the low D sung at the end of each verse was delivered 'acceptably' but without Karen's usual power. Nevertheless, the track remains one of their best recordings, and would've surely been a hit had it been released as a single. But it *has* found its way onto several *best of* compilations.

That year, the band appeared on a Bob Hope TV special, exchanging zingers with their host before miming to 'A Song For You' edited minus the saxophone solo.

'Top Of The World' (Richard Carpenter, John Bettis)
Single A-side b/w 'Heather'
Release date: 17 September 1973
Charts: US: 1, UK: 5
This international number one single began life as a passing comment from John Bettis, who was on tour with the band and their two hired Lear Jets Carpenter 1 and Carpenter 2. As Bettis recounted on the ITV documentary *The Nation's Favourite Carpenters Song,* he looked out the window mid-flight and remarked on how they were 'on top of the world', to which Richard replied, 'That's a good title!'. Bettis worked on an early version with musician Kerry Chater (the writer of the 1981 Carpenters single '(Want You) Back In My Life Again'). As that version was never completed, Bettis and Richard wrote a new version.

For this upbeat country tune, Karen supplied cheerful vocals, Tony Peluso played finger-picked guitar, and Hal Blaine played brushes. Richard came up with a memorable Wurlitzer electric piano riff, and other details like the ascending pattern after the word 'heaven', and the flurry of keyboard notes illustrating the line 'Something in the wind has learnt my name'. A key part of the sound is the pedal steel guitar – played by Red Rhodes on the album, and Buddy Emmons on the subsequent single. These ingredients added up to one of the most catchy and joyful songs the band had created so far, yet according to Lennox and May's interviews with Richard, he states that both he and Karen originally thought the song was no more than '...a nice album cut'. However, in the months following the release, they noticed the song was being mentioned in album reviews, how concert audiences cheered when the title was announced, and how much fan mail the song was generating. Taking the hint, in September 1972, the duo announced from the stage at Las Vegas' Riviera Hotel that 'Top Of The World' was their forthcoming single. A&M immediately talked them out of it, concerned that four singles had already been taken from the album. Forced to accept A&M's decision, Richard was frustrated further when country singer Lynn Anderson took a near-identical version to number 2 in the country chart, and 74 on the *Billboard* Hot 100.

Meanwhile, in Japan, their regional affiliate label decided to issue the tracks as a single, which went gold. Labels in Australia and New Zealand followed suit, and the song hit number 1 in both countries. A&M were at last persuaded, and the track was remixed with Karen replacing the original lead vocal she was never happy with, and Richard re-recording his Wurlitzer part. Tony Peluso played extra guitar fills, and Buddy Emmons added the new pedal steel, including a revised introduction.

The single was issued in September 1973, foreshadowing the *Singles 1969-1973* compilation. It was a case of better late than never, and the single became their second US *Billboard* number 1. Their first outright country single, its success also helped John Bettis' career as a country songwriter in Nashville.

The song was popular around the world, with international singers recording translations into Danish, Dutch, Finnish, Hebrew and other languages. The tune has also been adapted for the worship song 'There's a Life That's Deeper than Our Mind' that is popular in Korean Christian churches.

In March 2023, Indian film composer MM Keeravaani brought 'Top Of The World' to the Academy Awards ceremony, changing the lyric into an acceptance speech on winning the Best Original Song Oscar for 'Naatu Naatu' from 2022's *RRR*. Richard and two of his daughters sent congratulations by singing their own updated version of the song in an Instagram video.

'Hurting Each Other' (Peter Udell, Gary Geld)
Single A-side b/w 'Maybe It's You'
Release date: 23 December 1971
Charts: US: 2, UK: -
Composed by the team that wrote Brian Hyland's 1962 hit 'Sealed with a Kiss', 'Hurting Each Other' was first recorded by Jimmy Clanton in 1965, but that version failed to chart. The same year, Canadian act Chad Allan & The Expressions took the song to 19 in Canada. That band would later become The Guess Who, famous for 'American Woman'. The Walker Brothers issued 'Hurting Each Other' as an album track before Ruby and the Romantics released their 1969 single. It was that version that Richard heard on KRLA,

and felt certain it could be a hit. Unfortunately, The Romantics single reached only 113. Richard was reminded of the song a few years later when playing through some similar chords at a soundcheck, and he decided the Carpenters should attempt to turn it into a hit.

The Carpenters' arrangement eschews the introduction, going directly to the opening lines. Several elements are added to heighten the drama of the chorus. Karen's vocal is double-tracked, beginning from the pre-chorus line 'Tell me why then'. On the next words, 'Why should it be', the strings double her melody, and timpani drums are added at the second chorus. Another step was to follow each chorus line with a dramatic drum roll, as borrowed from the Chad Allan version. And, of course, Karen switches to a higher vocal range, hitting the song's highest note – A – every time she sings the word 'each'. According to Richard, Karen's throat problems struck again here, requiring several takes to accurately place the higher notes: something she would normally do with no trouble. Nevertheless, Karen still insisted on singing multiple overdubs of the backing vocal phrase 'We are', wanting to make them not only 'huge' but 'huger', as reported in Lucy O'Brien's biography of Karen.

A film clip was shot at A&M Studio B in early 1972. The duo were also filmed in the studio recording their backing vocals as part of a TV interview with Californian news reporter Jerry Dunphy. This must have been a recreation of their recording session, since TV filming took place in January, after the single's release, to be broadcast in early February. Producer Jack Daugherty can be seen at the studio controls, and the film also includes a tour of the Downey, CA home the duo bought for themselves and their parents.

The song became an international hit, though strangely, it didn't chart in the UK. In the US, it was kept from number 1 by Harry Nilsson's 'Without You': an even more melodramatic song.

The version issued in 1973 on *The Singles 1969-1973*, excludes the tambourine and some timpani, but includes an intake of breath from Karen at the start. This was omitted in the 1990 remix but given greater prominence in the 1991 mix. The 1990 remix gave the track stereo piano, new reverb and heavier bass.

'It's Going To Take Some Time' (Carole King, Toni Stern)
Single A-side b/w 'Flat Baroque'
Release date: 13 April 1972
Charts: US: 12 (Not released in the UK)
This song was written for Carole King's third solo album *Music*. It was released in late 1971 as the follow-up to her runaway success *Tapestry*, which was recorded at A&M's studio B in January 1971 while the Carpenters worked on their eponymous 'Tan' album. The Carpenters were there again when King recorded her *Music* album, and heard some of the tracks.

The Carpenters' version changes the tempo and key, starting a half-step lower in C, but modulating up to the key of King's original by the end. They kept the opening piano figure, which might have inspired the opening of Chicago's 1976 hit 'If You Leave Me Now'.

Tim Weisberg was hired to play bass flute, along with Bob Messenger, who played alto flute. Messenger delivers a jazz-like flute solo, which ends with the equally jazz-like D13 chord as the song transitions to the new key of Db. According to Craig Halstead's book *Carpenters: All the Top 40 Hits*, embellishments like these led Carole King to exclaim, 'You've made mine sound like a demo!'. Perhaps they *had*, but when this single failed to reach the top 10, Richard felt that releasing 'Top Of The World' would've been a smarter move and could've increased album sales by another 2,000,000. Luckily, the next single was to improve matters.

'Goodbye To Love' (Richard Carpenter, John Bettis)
Single A-side b/w 'Crystal Lullaby'
Release date: 19 June 1972
Charts: US: 7, UK: 9

The idea for this classic came one night in London as Richard watched the old black-and-white Bing Crosby film *Rhythm on the River*. The plot concerned songwriting, and referred to a hit called 'Goodbye To Love', though the song was never actually heard in the film. Inspired, Richard soon had the melody, the opening four lines, and the idea for the choral ending. The song was completed with John Bettis in early 1972.

The music itself is relatively sweet and pleasant, yet the lyric is incredibly bleak and stands beside such gloomy 1970s songs as Terry Jacks' 'Seasons in the Sun' or Gilbert O'Sullivan's 'Alone Again (Naturally)'. The music conceivably lessens the impact of lines like 'No one ever cared if I should live or die' and 'Loneliness and emptiness will be my only friend', though subtle tension is created by subdividing the eight-bar verse into groups of five and three, and from the persistent pedal note that runs through a lot of the verse.

Another kind of tension exists in the long phrases Karen delivers in a single breath. Given the slow tempo, it's an amazing – if overlooked – feat that she can add vocal colouring and nuance to protracted lines like 'Time and time again the chance for love has passed me by, and all I know of love is how to live without it' and the equally extensive 'And though it's not the easy way, I guess I've always known I'd say goodbye to love'. Acknowledging her exceptional skill, Richard has noted how most other singers break these lines up in order to catch their breath. The duo recorded the three-part 'Aah' backing vocals at the end after several glasses of wine at the popular music industry hangout Martoni's of Hollywood.

Tony Peluso's iconic fuzz guitar solo was played on a 1957 Gibson ES-335 with an Electro Harmonix Big Muff pedal. He begins by repeating the first five bars of the verse melody before soaring – in Richard's words – 'off into the stratosphere'. According to a 2020 article by Tony Havers on the udiscovermusic website, Peluso began by playing more gentle ideas before Richard urged him to 'burn it up'. The solo was then captured in a few takes, which were later compiled together. Peluso had been playing in the Carpenters' opening act, and was soon invited to join full-time. The inclusion of fuzz guitar was a novel move, and proved to be too much for some fans, who sent hate mail accusing the duo of selling out and turning into a rock group. In time, the song became recognised as an early example of a power ballad.

The single went top five in five countries and top ten in the US and UK. Subsequent remixes have restored Karen's opening breath, which was originally removed because her microphone had picked up Richard's count-in via her headset. The original count in can be heard in the remix on *The Nation's Favourite Carpenters' Songs* (UK) and the *Anthology* (Japan).

'Intermission' (Richard Carpenter)

Side one ends with a mischievous take on an 18th-century religious motet. The overlapping fugal lines of Antonio Lotti's 'Crucifixus' allow for a lengthy setup to a punchline about going to the *bathroom* (pronounced with an upper-class English accent for added good measure). The duo had learnt this piece while choir members at CSULB, and would sometimes sing it while working in the studio. 'Crucifuxus' was originally arranged for eight voices, though this adaptation uses just four.

'Bless The Beasts And Children' (Perry Botkin Jr., Barry De Vorzon)
Single A-side b/w 'Superstar'
Release date: 12 August 1971
Charts: US: 67

While recording the *Carpenters* (Tan) album, Richard received a phone call from film director and producer Stanley Kramer, the maker of *It's a Mad, Mad, Mad, Mad World* (1963) and *Guess Who's Coming to Dinner* (1967). Kramer wanted the Carpenters to record the theme song of his next project, *Bless the Beasts and Children* – the story of six troubled teenage boys who attend an Arizona summer camp and save a herd of buffalos. Barry De Vorzon's songs had been recorded by Marty Robbins and Johnny Burnette, while Botkin had worked as an arranger for Harry Nilsson, Carly Simon and Barbra Streisand.

The song starts with the verse melody played by Doug Strawn on a clarinet, sent through the oboe setting on a Gibson Maestro Woodwind Sound System, an electronic unit (also used by Frank Zappa on his 1969 album *Uncle Meat*). Earle Dumler replaced this part with a real oboe for the 1985 remix. On the film soundtrack version, Richard played this melody on the Wurlitzer electric piano with tremolo, creating a vibraphone-like sound.

As the verse begins, Karen adopts a beseeching tone to sing the prayer-like lyric, aided by choir-like backing vocals and a Hammond organ. A squeak from the studio door being opened during Karen's vocal take can be heard near the end of verse one under the phrase 'They have no voice'.

Hal Blaine played the bridge drums, though his part was re-recorded for the 1985 remix. The 1991 remix ends with a piano chord rather than fading out, as heard on *The Essential Collection: 1965-1997*.

The song was first released in August 1971 as the B-side to 'Superstar', receiving so much radio airplay of its own that the single became listed as a double A-side on the *Billboard* chart. 13 weeks after that single's release, 'Bless the Beasts and Children' began an eight-week chart run as an A-side, reaching number 67. It was nominated for the Academy Award for Best Original Song, and the duo performed it at the April ceremony, though the Oscar went to Isaac Hayes for 'Theme from Shaft'.

'Bless the Beasts and Children' was the only Carpenters recording on the film soundtrack. Interestingly, they were offered two even bigger film themes at this time: '(Where Do I Begin?) Love Story' and 'Speak Softly Love (Love Theme from *The Godfather*)'. But they considered neither a good fit, and turned them down. Both became hits for Andy Williams instead.

'Flat Baroque' (Richard Carpenter)
This instrumental dates back to The Richard Carpenter Trio's 1966 RCA Victor demo, though the band included the song in their 1970 radio broadcasts for *Your Navy Presents*.

The piece blends jazz elements (such as Karen's brushes) with classical stylings, such as the Gavotte-inspired 2/4 time signature. Bassoon player Norm Herzberg trades counterpoint melodies with Earle Dumler on oboe. Richard demonstrates his piano skills, playing a solo with plenty of decorative turns and trills, and the track makes a companion piece to the following 'Piano Picker'.

The version on the B-side of 'It's Going to Take Some Time' was remixed with different stereo placements to add depth.

'Piano Picker' (Randy Edelman)
Following a piano showcase, we now get the backstory on how those skills were learnt. With self-deprecatory humour, Richard recounts his years spent in dedicated practice at the expense of social activities like sports and dating. Though the lyric corresponds closely with Richard's experience, this is really the autobiography of singer-songwriter and pianist Randy Edelman, who included the song on his eponymous 1971 debut album. Artists like Barry Manilow, Bing Crosby and Abba's Agnetha Fältskog all covered his songs, and the Carpenters later recorded Edelman's 'I Can't Make Music' and 'You'.

Edelman began his version with 90 seconds of light classical piano, while the Carpenters' version goes straight to the verse. Unfortunately, the simple piano accompaniment exposes Richard's sibilant lisp, though it's helpfully masked when his voice is double-tracked later in the song. The chorus differs from Edelman's original by adding a vocalese section, the same melody then repeated by strings and piano. Richard lists his typical practice routine of 'Hanon, Czerny, Bach' after the second verse.

The song became a concert feature, and the lyric was eventually adapted to tell Richard's personal musical history, with references to Les Paul and learning songs by ear from the radio. In verse two, Karen is introduced as a 'tomboy Krupa who sang a little Como', referring to jazz drummer Gene Krupa and singer Perry Como. At this point in the concert, Karen appeared onstage to play a show-stopping drum solo during a medley of the Gershwin tunes 'Strike Up the Band', 'S'Wonderful' and 'Fascinating Rhythm'. For this section of the show, Karen wore a t-shirt saying 'Lead Sister'. The phrase came from a translation error when the band were interviewed for a Japanese magazine. This medley can be heard on the 1976 *Live at the Palladium* album, and can also be seen in the BBC concert *Live at the New London Theatre,* filmed on 25 November 1976 at Covent Garden.

'I Won't Last a Day Without You' (Paul Williams, Roger Nichols)
Single A-side b/w 'Goodbye To Love'
Release date: UK: September 1972
Charts: UK: 49
A-side b/w 'One Love'
Release date: US: 25 March 1974
Charts: US: 11, UK: 32 (1974)
This became the album's sixth single, topping the charts in Hong Kong. However, the story is circuitous and troubled. The Williams and Nichols' original demo was of just two verses and a chorus. In the studio, Karen requested the addition of a bridge and third verse, and the situation became tense as the new version was delivered just one day before the scheduled recording. Nichols was unhappy to learn that Richard had made changes to the melody and chords. The bridge Nichols wrote can be heard on the versions by Barbra Streisand, Diana Ross and Paul Williams. The Carpenters opened their previous two albums with Williams/Nichols songs, and this was the last of their songs the duo would record, as the songwriting pair split shortly after.

The sessions became even more fraught as Karen struggled to double her chorus vocal. What would've normally been a quick process required repeated takes as Karen's throat was painful due to, what later turned out to be, sores on her vocal cords.

Though the duo considered the song to be just an album track, the UK branch of A&M chose to release it as a single with 'Goodbye To Love' as the B-side. It entered the UK charts at 49, but the following week, the label changed their mind and made the A-side 'Goodbye To Love', which reached the top 10. The proper single release of 'I Won't Last a Day Without You' didn't occur until March 1974, when it was issued in the US at the request of the RKO radio station chain. For this release, Tony Peluso added new guitar parts to the song's second half, injecting the track with new life and helping it reach 11 in *Billboard*. In 1991, this version was remixed and can be heard on the compilations *Carpenters Gold, The Essential Collection: 1965-1997* and *The Nation's Favourite Carpenters' Songs* (UK).

'Crystal Lullaby' (Richard Carpenter, John Bettis)
Another song reclaimed from the Spectrum era, the lyric describes a young girl's dreams as her father's lullaby puts her to sleep. The duo share the lead vocal, and in the final section, the narration switches to the first person. One of the album's lighter pieces, it's a contrast to the following heavyhearted ballad.

'Road Ode' (Gary Sims, Danny Woodhams)
This was written by Carpenters band members Gary Sims (guitar) and Danny Woodhams (bass) while on tour. The doleful lyrics compare the glamour of performing with the loneliness of 'empty motel rooms' and 'roads of sorrows'. Karen softly confides the routine details of life on the road over a soft backing, before the chorus breaks into a funky rhythm, Bob Messenger later playing a flute solo. Despite the gloomy lyric, Richard's recollection is that the group had a lot of fun on tour, regardless of the heavy schedule.

In 1990, the piano, bass and flute solo were re-recorded for a remix intended for future compilations: including the three-CD US set *The Complete Singles* (2015).

'A Song For You (Reprise)' (Leon Russell)
Entering on a harp glissando on the same chord as the prior song's final chord, this title track reprise fades in from a tunnel of reverb and makes a neat bookend for the album.

Now And Then (1973)

Personnel:
Karen Carpenter: vocals, drums
Richard Carpenter: vocals, keyboards, orchestrator, arranger
Joe Osborn: bass
Tony Peluso: lead guitar, DJ voice (6)
Gary Sims: guitar
Buddy Emmons, Jay Dee Maness: steel guitar
Bob Messenger: flute, tenor saxophone
Doug Strawn: baritone sax
Tom Scott: recorder
Earle Dumler: oboe, bass oboe, English horn
Hal Blaine: drums (4)
The Jimmy Joyce Children's Chorus: backing vocals (1)
Special thanks to Ron Gorow
Produced by Richard and Karen Carpenter
Engineered by Ray Gerhardt and Roger Young
Recorded at A&M Records, Hollywood, California
Release date: 1 May 1973
Label: A&M
Charts: US: 2, UK: 2
Running Time 37:46

As the hits kept coming, so did the promotional engagements. Richard recalls playing over 170 concerts in 1972, and a similar amount in 1973. On top of this came in-person appearances and TV shows, yet Richard adds the band still enjoyed playing live. They even caught the attention of President Richard Nixon, who – according to Randy Schmidt's Karen biography – described them as 'Young America at its very best'. Nixon was eager to improve his image in light of continuing Vietnam War protests, and in August 1972, he invited the duo to the White House for a photo opportunity, and again in May 1973 to perform at a state function.

In summer 1972, the duo added a nostalgic medley of 1950s and 1960s hits to their live show. Rock and roll was having a revival at the time, thanks in part to doo-wop group Sha Na Na, who appeared at Woodstock in 1969, and also to the musical *Grease*, which began a Broadway run in June 1972. A similar revival was hitting the UK with glam rock, and the return of the Teddy Boy fashion style.

Pushed for time as usual when selecting songs to record, Richard fashioned an oldies medley based on the live show to fill side two, inspired perhaps by The Beatles' 1969 *Abbey Road* medley. The medley songs were linked by DJ announcements modelled on the then-emerging oldies radio format of stations like Arizona's KOOL-FM in and KRTH in Los Angeles. Having chosen eight of their favourite oldies, the duo decided that the best way to capture the spirit of the past would be to stay as close as possible to the original arrangements.

Now And Then was the Carpenters' first self-produced album. Since their debut, Richard had grown increasingly frustrated with reviews praising their producer, Jack Daugherty, for the high audio quality. Richard felt the credit for that belonged to him, while Daugherty's contributions were more administrative, booking musicians and studio time. At Richard's insistence, Daugherty was dismissed from his A&M position, and promptly responded by suing the label, resulting in a lawsuit that took nine years to resolve. Though Daugherty eventually lost this court battle, it was a pyrrhic victory for A&M.

Another personnel change was to replace their live drummer, Jim Anthony, with Cubby O'Brien: a former *Mickey Mouse Club* Mouseketeer. But in the studio, Karen played on the new album with the exception of 'Jambalaya (On the Bayou)', the backing track of which had been recorded with Hal Blaine the previous year. Some sources suggest that Blaine also plays on 'Yesterday Once More', though this is credited to Karen in the sleeve notes. Whatever the case, Blaine's influence was felt throughout the oldies medley, him having been the original drummer on five of the eight songs – 'Fun, Fun, Fun', 'Da Doo Ron Ron', 'Dead Man's Curve', 'Johnny Angel' and 'The Night Has a Thousand Eyes'.

Agnes Carpenter suggested the album title, to describe the mixture of new and old songs. Extending the family connection, the cover photo was taken outside the family home at 9828 Newville Avenue, Downey, California, where Karen was to tragically collapse and lose consciousness ahead of her death in 1983.

The album cover began as yet another hastily conceived idea from the label's marketing department. The original concept was simply to photograph the siblings standing in front of the house. Richard was astounded at the inanity of this, proposing instead that they try some shots of the pair sitting in his car: a red 1972 Ferrari 365 GTB/4, popularly known as the Daytona, following Ferrari's success at the Daytona race track. Luckily, this suggestion produced not only a distinctive album cover, but one that tied in neatly with the album concept of driving around listening to an oldies station. The photo was taken with a wide-angle lens, and printed across three panels in a luxurious double gatefold or trifold design. The colours and textures were enhanced through additional airbrushing by Design Maru studio. But Len Freas' inside-cover portraits were less successful, with Karen's face glowing an unnatural shade of orange.

The album itself was a hit, reaching two on *Billboard*, going two-times platinum and yielding two hit singles. Success was in the air, but there were changes on the horizon.

'Sing' (Joe Raposo)
Single A-side b/w 'Drusilla Penny'
Release date: 13 January 1973
Charts: US: 3, UK: 55

Side one consists of entirely new songs, forming the album's 'Now' side. It opens with a song written in 1971 for the educational children's TV show *Sesame Street*. Writer Joe Raposo wrote a simple and direct lyric that a young audience could easily understand, mostly using one-syllable words. The song's first release was as a tie-in single performed by the show's actors, but other artists were quick to realise its appeal to all ages. Peggy Lee and Trini Lopez both released versions on albums; Lopez in Spanish. Barbra Streisand included 'Sing' in a live medley with 'Make Your Own Kind of Music', releasing it as a single in 1972 under the title 'Sing a Song', reaching number 92.

Richard states that neither he nor Karen knew the song until they were guests on a 1973 ABC TV special called *Robert Young with the Young*. There, they performed 'Sing' with a group of children, actors Sandy Duncan and Arte Johnson, and the show's host Robert Young. Richard was immediately taken with the song, and was planning an arrangement before he even left the TV studio. He thought it reminded him of 'Getting to Know You' from the musical *The King and I*. It might also be said to recall 'Do-Re-Mi' from *The Sound of Music*.

In the Carpenters' version, the catchy refrain is heard first on a recorder, then a flugelhorn. Richard adjusted the phrase from earlier versions to end more conclusively on the dominant note. In the second verse, recorders play a counter melody, and the Jimmy Joyce Children's Choir join in from verse three onwards. But the choir's singing wasn't quite good enough, so Karen doubled their parts in her upper register. Richard played on A&M's piano B, which was Carole King's preferred piano, though Richard's preference was for piano A.

Richard's instinct told him the song should be a single, though A&M were initially resistant. He was proven right when the single hit 3 in the US and was certified gold, receiving two Grammy nominations. The catchy song and its simple message travelled well overseas, reaching the charts in a further ten countries and inspiring covers in at least seven languages. At the request of their international affiliate labels, the duo sang a Spanish version that was released in Mexico in 1973. The alternate version, 'Canta/Sing' has Karen singing one line in English, and can be heard on the 1991 *From the Top* compilation.

'This Masquerade' (Leon Russell)

The album moves on to the complexity of adult relationships, a sultry flute replacing the innocent-sounding recorder of the prior song. According to Lennox and May's book on the Carpenters, Richard modified the flute sound with an Eventide Octaver effect that electronically adds a lower octave to each note, though this was removed for subsequent remixes. Karen gives one of her finest vocal performances, her smooth voice gliding over the gentle Latin rhythm and atmospheric cocktail-jazz piano. The buzzing percussion sound heard in the introduction is a vibraslap.

The verse chords descend while Karen climbs from a low F to G an octave up, while the bass holds a steady root note. The 'mas' of 'masquerade' is sung on a flattened 5th blue note that sounds slightly askew, just like the couple's relationship in the lyric. The bridge changes key twice before climbing back to the home key of F minor. Following Richard's piano solo, Bob Messenger plays a dazzling flute solo, returning to solo over the outro.

The group had included a Leon Russell song on their last two albums, though this was the last song of his they'd record. Richard felt that 'This Masquerade' would make a good hit single, but at almost five minutes in length, it was too long, and he couldn't bring himself to edit it. This cleared the way for George Benson's version to hit the Top 10 in 1976, courageously editing his eight-minute album version.

'Heather' (Johnny Pearson)

The album proceeds with this light instrumental piece from English composer Johnny Pearson. Pearson had helped produce the Carpenters' *Live at the BBC* TV show in 1971, and he also led the orchestra on the UK TV chart show *Top of the Pops* throughout the 1970s. He returned as the Carpenters' band leader on their *Talk of The Town* BBC concert in 1974.

This minor-key tune was originally titled 'Autumn Reverie', but was renamed 'Heather' by John Bettis. It first appeared on the 1968 KPM library music album *Gentle Sounds,* though Richard heard it first in a TV ad for the health supplement Geritol. The piece was later used as background music in the 1970s British TV series *All Creatures Great and Small*, for which Pearson also composed the theme tune.

In the Carpenters' arrangement, the melody is passed between piano and woodwinds over a bed of strings and harp, recalling the easy-listening albums of Mantovani, Ronnie Aldrich or Percy Faith.

'Jambalaya (On The Bayou)' (Hank Williams)
Single A-side b/w 'Mr Guder'
Release date: US: 15 February 1974 (Not released in UK)
Charts: US: 12

This enduring favourite was originally a 1952 number-one country hit for Hank Williams with His Drifting Cowboys. It's been covered many times, and Richard knew it best from Jo Stafford's 1952 hit.

At least nine other artists issued the song around the time of the Carpenters' recording, including The Nitty Gritty Dirt Band, Shocking Blue, John Fogerty's Blue Ridge Rangers and Leon Russell. The Carpenters' recording was a hit in several countries but was not a single in the US. It has since been included on several compilations, with a remix in 1991.

The song has just two chords, and is based on a traditional tune known variously as 'Gran Prairie', 'Gran' Texas' and 'Big Texas'. The Carpenters version starts with flute, adding various ingredients – like a guitar solo, pedal steel and cries of 'Yeeha!'. Running short of time in the studio, chorus two's multitracked backing vocals were copied over onto the third. This was not standard practice for the group, and Richard said it was the only time they did it.

A certain amount of the song's appeal comes from its uncommon lyric, which uses French creole dialect to describe a big Louisiana-style family party, with terms like 'pirogue' and 'filé gumbo' and local family names like Thibodaux and Fountaineaux.

'I Can't Make Music' (Randy Edelman)

This was a song that Edelman had played live when opening for the Carpenters. Starting simply, this song builds to its climax at the final chorus with piano, strings and a pipe-organ sound. It ends softly with harmonica, and violin played by Jimmy Getzoff.

'Yesterday Once More' (Richard Carpenter, John Bettis)
Single A-side b/w 'Road Ode'
Release date: 15 May 1973
Charts: US: 2, UK: 2

Opening side two – the 'Then' side – is the song that became the group's biggest-selling hit globally, and Richard has claimed it to be his favourite of all his compositions. The idea for the song came to him one day driving along Highland Avenue to the A&M lot. He heard the melody and first four lyric lines in his head, and passed these on to John Bettis, explaining how the song would introduce the album's oldies medley.

As the recording deadline approached, Bettis hadn't completed the lyric, so he and Richard teamed up to finish the job, searching for old song titles to include in the lyric. When the result sounded contrived and awkward, Karen talked them out of the idea, but Bettis insisted on keeping the 'Sha la la' and 'Shing-a-ling-a-ling' chorus phrases. These words were only intended as placeholders, but ultimately, they provided a more vivid link to the musical styles of the past. One classic song title *did* make it into the lyric – or almost – as the line 'All the oldies but goodies' is close to the 1961 doo-wop hit 'Those Oldies but Goodies (Remind Me of You)' by Little Caesar and the Romans.

The single reached number two in the US (kept from the top spot by Jim Croce's 'Bad, Bad Leroy Brown'). It was their most successful UK single, reaching number two. The song was remixed for the single, adding guitar and oboe parts. The 1985 remix had a heavier sound.

'Medley'
'Fun Fun Fun' (Brian Wilson, Mike Love)
With a rev of engines, we're ready at the start line to race through eight classics from 1961-1964. This was the era of teen idols, girl groups, surf bands and Motown soul, just ahead of the British Invasion. Richard was 14 in 1961, while Karen was 11, both keeping their ears open to the music of

the day. Richard has often cited the influence of the 'three Bs': The Beatles, Bacharach and The Beach Boys. Having already recorded songs by the first two, the duo could now pay homage to the third, whose close-harmony vocals had been such an influence. Over the roar of motor engines, guitarist Tony Peluso lets rip with the Chuck Berry-inspired intro, and the band starts up the driving rhythm. Taking the vocal for the first number, Richard – an automobile enthusiast – gets to sing about Ford Thunderbirds, of which he later owned three. Skipping verse two, we go straight to his Wurlitzer solo, and on to the denouement where the teenage racer gets caught by her parents. Karen performs the theremin-like falsetto melody on the outro, as Peluso assumes the role of a fast-talking oldies-station DJ, introducing the next number...

'The End Of The World' (Arthur Kent, Sylvia Dee)

... which is a country/pop ballad in 12/8 time, made famous in 1963 by Skeeter Davis. Though it's about the end of a love affair, songwriter Sylvia Dee was actually moved to write the words following the death of her father. Davis' version hit number one on *Billboard*'s Easy Listening chart, and two on the Hot 100, where it was kept from number one by Ruby and the Romantics' 'Our Day Will Come': another song included in this medley. At the age of 13, Karen made one of her earliest public performances singing 'The End of the World', at an outdoor talent show in Downey, with Richard on piano. As the song reaches its end, the pedal steel ends on a high E, as Karen drops to an E at the low end of her vocal range.

'Da Doo Ron Ron (When He Walked Me Home)' (Jeff Barry, Ellie Greenwich, Phil Spector)

Tony Peluso, as DJ, introduces this cover of The Crystals' number-3 1963 hit. The songwriters Barry, Greenwich and Spector also wrote 'Be My Baby', 'Then He Kissed Me', 'Chapel of Love' and 'River Deep – Mountain High'. The nonsense title syllables were originally intended as placeholders, but Spector kept them as they didn't distract from the overall storyline of young love.

The Carpenters' arrangement is on a more modest scale than Spector's trademark Wall-of-Sound productions, but achieves a similar rhythmic effect. Karen's voice is multitracked, singing all the Crystals' verse harmonies, before Richard joins on the chorus. This version cut the number of verses, adding a new saxophone solo and contemporary guitar solo at the end. The DJ reappears, presenting an impossibly difficult 'mystery voice' competition, and introducing the next number.

'Dead Man's Curve' (Jan Berry, Roger Christian, Brian Wilson, Artie Kornfeld)

This is an infamous death song from 1963, released by surf rockers Jan and Dean. It tells the story of a doomed car race along Sunset Boulevard in Los

Angeles. The song was written by group member Jan Berry, Brian Wilson of The Beach Boys, car racer and DJ Roger Christian (who had co-written 'Little Deuce Coupe') and Artie Kornfeld: a member of The Changin' Times, and co-writer of The Cowsills 1967 hit 'The Rain, the Park and Other Things'. Coincidentally, Jan and Dean had also released singles on Joe Osborn's Magic Lamp label that issued Karen's first solo single 'Looking for Love'.

Richard takes the lead vocal for this second car-related song in the medley, picking up the story from verse two. The first verse would've introduced the models of the two cars in the race: a Jaguar XKE and Corvette Stingray. (Richard lists a 1966 Stingray in his online inventory of classic cars in his private collection.) The race ends when the Jaguar crashes at Dead Man's Curve – Jan and Dean's original version eerily foreshadowing the real-life tragedy of Jan Berry, who suffered brain damage after crashing his Corvette Stingray in 1966 while driving in the vicinity of Dead Man's Curve.

Skid and crash effects are added at the end for good measure as we segue from fatal car accident to angels.

'Johnny Angel' (Lyn Duddy, Lee Pockriss)
Songwriter Lee Pockriss' extensive credits include Perry Como's 'Catch a Falling Star', Brian Hyland's 'Itsy Bitsy Teenie Weenie Yellow Polkadot Bikini', and songs for TV's *Sesame Street* and Chuck Jones' animated 1970 feature *The Phantom Tollbooth*.

The introduction would normally require four singers, but with the magic of multitracking, it begins here with four overlapping parts by Karen. A few lyric lines were cut, but the song is otherwise intact, down to the nonsense backing vocal syllables 'Sha-dan Sha-dan' and the angelic choir at the end of the bridge.

'The Night Has A Thousand Eyes' (Benjamin Weisman, Dorothy Wayne, Marilynn Garrett)
This perky number was a top-3 hit for Bobby Vee in 1962. Benjamin Weisman is perhaps the best-known of its writers, having written 'Wooden Heart' and other songs for Elvis Presley. The song title comes from 19th-century English poet Francis William Bourdillon, and has also been used to title a novel and its film adaptation, not to mention the jazz standard based on that film's theme.

Starting with a military snare roll calling us to attention, the song sets off on the bumpy verse rhythm. On this song, Richard sings his final lead vocal for a Carpenters album, with the exception of the Christmas records. The major-key verse switches to a minor chorus, and Karen's drums switch to a busy Latin rhythm. Hal Blaine played drums on Bobby Vee's hit recording.

At the end, our zany DJ takes a call from hapless quiz contestant Mark Rudolph, who was Karen and Richard's real first cousin. Outtake bloopers from this segment are included on the compilations *From the Top* and *The Essential Collection: 1965-1997*.

'Our Day Will Come' (Bob Hilliard, Mort Garson)

Maintaining the Latin feel, this track floats along on a *bossa nova* rhythm, with Richard's cocktail piano Karen's rapturous vocal. A hit for Ruby and the Romantics in 1963, this optimistic song has been a popular choice for many artists, including Doris Day, Carpenters' songwriter Roger Nichols and Amy Winehouse. The music was written by Mort Garson – an arranger for The Lettermen, Esther Phillips, and The Hollyridge Strings. Lyricist Bob Hilliard also wrote the words for 'The Coffee Song', 'In the Wee Small Hours of the Morning', and songs from the 1951 Disney musical *Alice in Wonderland*.

With one last sign-off from the DJ, we approach the medley's final golden oldie.

'One Fine Day' (Carole King, Gerry Goffin)

This optimistic 1963 song was originally a hit for The Chiffons: also known for 'Sweet Talkin' Guy' and 'He's So Fine'. The husband-and-wife team of Gerry Goffin and Carole King were songwriters based in New York's Brill Building, and their other hits included 'Halfway to Paradise' and 'Will You Still Love Me Tomorrow'.

The track opens with insistent piano notes, taken up by Karen's 'Shoobie doobie' vocals. The saxophone solo is a close match to The Chiffons' original recording. Richard has noted that this song fortuitously matched the key of the reprise that follows.

'Yesterday Once More (Reprise)' (Richard Carpenter, John Bettis)

The medley is bookended with this reprise of the side's opening song, leaving one last bittersweet remembrance of things past. Karen repeats the opening line while the backing vocals chant 'So fine': a phrase from the chorus. The reverb and phasing effects grow stronger as memories of the past float by, such as a vocal phrase from Neil Sedaka's 1962 hit 'Breaking Up is Hard to Do'. Attentive listeners will have noticed Richard playing this phrase four bars earlier. Just after the Sedaka line, a groan sound is heard, which apparently appeared during the mastering stage, much to the bemusement of mastering engineer Bernie Grundman.

Related Tracks

'Morinaga Hi-Crown Chocolate Commercial' (Koji Makaino)

This soundtrack for a Japanese TV advertisement was recorded in 1974 at A&M Studio D. The ad showed Karen and Richard dressed in white walking on a beach, and sitting beside an abandoned building inspecting wildflowers. This was neither their first nor last advertisement, having previously appeared in TV and radio commercials for Morton's Potato Chips in 1971, recorded while on tour in Canada supporting Engelbert Humperdinck. Further ads are discussed in later chapters. The Morinaga commercial is included on the compilation *The Essential Collection: 1965-1997*.

'Santa Claus Is Comin' To Town' (Haven Gillespie, John Frederick Coots)
Single A-side b/w 'Merry Christmas, Darling'
Release date: US: 6 December 1974
Charts: US: -, UK: 37

Coots – who wrote the music to this well-known 1934 Christmas song – also wrote the haunting ballad 'You Go to My Head'. 'Santa Claus is Comin' to Town' has been recorded by a host of artists, including Les Paul, Skeeter Davis, The Crystals on Phil Spector's 1963 Christmas Album, and The Beach Boys on theirs. Unlike most other versions, the Carpenters' arrangement is a ballad. They recorded the rhythm track with drummer Hal Blaine in 1972, but didn't have time to complete the recording until September 1974, when Karen successfully sang it in one take.

Another artist to record the song was Perry Como: a favourite of Agnes Carpenter. The Carpenters promoted the single as guests on *Perry Como's Christmas Show* in 1974. Karen sang 'Sleep Well, Little Children' with Como, while Richard performed 'Carol of the Bells' with a choir. There was a group rendition of 'It's Christmas Time' leading into 'It's Beginning to Look a Lot Like Christmas', and a medley of Carpenters and Perry Como songs.

The single wasn't given a *Billboard* chart position due to a rule stating that Christmas songs couldn't be counted in the usual singles charts.

'Carpenters/Como Medley' (From *Perry Como's Christmas Show* (1974)
This medley was included on the collection *As Time Goes By:* issued in Japan in 2001, and the US in 2004. The recording is 6:52 in length, comprising the entire medley as performed, though the TV broadcast was cut for time, skipping the first few minutes and opening on Como singing 'Close To You'.

The idea for the medley was for the artists to sing each other's hits, beginning with Karen singing the opening lines of 'Yesterday Once More', making a thematic link to the golden-oldies selection. The first is 'Magic Moments': a Bacharach/David song that was a hit for Como in 1957. It segues into their hit 'Sing'. Richard stands in for Como here since the microphone used in the TV studio did not pick up Como's vocals as clearly at this point.

Next comes Como's 1957 hit 'Catch a Falling Star' – co-written by Lee Pockriss who also co-wrote 'Johnny Angel' – which was included in the oldies medley on *Now And Then*. Como now enters the recording, singing 'Close To You', though Richard sings the opening line due to canned applause on the TV broadcast. Karen then sings Como's 1970 hit 'It's Impossible'.

After this, comes 'We've Only Just Begun', Richard standing in for Como again on certain lines. Karen sings with Como on his 1973 hit 'And I Love You So' (written by singer-songwriter Don Maclean). Richard now sings the country two-step 'Don't Let the Stars Get in Your Eyes': a hit for Como in 1952.

The medley returns to its opening theme, 'Yesterday Once More', and Richard replaces more of Como's lines, also correcting the line Como mistakenly sang as 'Every sing-a-ling-a-ling that *you* started to sing'. Richard inserts a line from 'Til the End of Time' (a Como recording from 1945) and Karen does the same with 'No Other Love Have I' (from the Rodgers and Hammerstein musical *Me and Juliet*): a hit for Como in 1953. The medley ends with Como singing the line, 'We've only just begun'.

Horizon (1975)

Personnel:
Karen Carpenter: vocals, drums
Richard Carpenter: vocals, keyboards, orchestrator, arranger
Joe Osborn: bass
Tony Peluso: guitar
Red Rhodes, Thad Maxwell: steel guitar
Bob Messenger: tenor saxophone
Doug Strawn: baritone sax
Tom Morgan: harmonica
Earle Dumler: oboe, English horn
Jim Gordon: drums
Gayle Levant: harp
Billy May: orchestrator and co-arranger (5)
Joe Mondragon: bass (5)
Alvin Stoller: drums (5)
Pete Jolly: keyboards (5)
Frank Flynn: vibes (5)
Bob Bain: guitar (5)
Jackie Ward, Mitch Gordon, John Bahler, Gene Merlino: backing vocals (5)
Special thanks to Ron Gorow
Produced by Richard Carpenter
Associate Producer: Karen Carpenter
Engineered by Ray Gerhardt, Roger Young and Dave Iveland
Recorded at A&M Records, Hollywood, California
Release date: 6 June 1975
Label: A&M
Charts: US: 13 UK: 1
Running Time 34:53

Following the release of the November-1973 compilation *The Singles 1969-1973*, 1974 saw only singles issued: 'I Won't Last a Day Without You', 'Santa Claus is Comin' to Town', and the most successful,'Please Mr. Postman', which reached number 1 in six countries, and the top 10 in another five.

But promotional duties continued, including presenting the Best New Artist award to Bette Midler at the Grammys in March, and appearing on the cover of *Rolling Stone* in July. The magazine gave the Carpenters a surprisingly sympathetic interview, portraying them with depth, and challenging their 'goody-four-shoes' image. Most of the year was spent on tour, playing over 200 US shows, visiting new countries like Sweden, Denmark, Belgium and the Netherlands, and returning to the UK and Japan. Televised concerts from 1974 included a performance for *Top Pop* in Amsterdam, a show at London's The Talk of the Town for the BBC, and a concert at Tokyo's Budokan in May (later issued on DVD). Selections from a three-night run at Osaka's Festival

Hall were issued in Japan on the 1975 King Records LP *Live in Japan*. Back in the US, an August televised concert titled *Evening at the Pops* saw the band perform with Arthur Fiedler and the Boston Pops Orchestra, including an overture of Carpenters tunes.

Tracking for the new *Horizon* began in September 1974, lasting into the early months of 1975 due to touring and TV commitments. Full use was made of A&M's new 24-track facilities in Studio D, and Richard was proud of the production quality. For once, the band were happy with their cover portrait, which depicted them looking natural in an outdoor setting. The mood was well-matched to the LP's mature and reflective songs, which many fans consider to be the band's best. Richard later stated that he had reservations about the album, considering it too 'sleepy' on account of the number of ballads. He has also described how the band's heavy promotional schedule was affecting his ability to make decisions in the studio. For one thing, this was their first album without a lead vocal from Richard.

Karen was also feeling the pressure, and her weight loss was now becoming noticeable. This didn't appear to affect her singing or drumming, and she still played drums on several tracks, including 'Please Mr Postman', while Jim Gordon played on the remainder.

Fans had waited two years for a new album. Even so, *Horizon* sold less than their previous albums, peaking at 13 on *Billboard*. It was their last album to reach the Top 20, and was the start of an overall decline in sales and chart positions. Richard regrets that *Horizon* wasn't released back in January when 'Please Mr Postman' was number one, though the album *did* eventually go platinum. It was received well overseas, where it spent five weeks at number one in the UK and Japan, and nine weeks at number one in Zimbabwe.

'Aurora' (Richard Carpenter, John Bettis)
The album begins and ends with the same short piece of music, picturing first a morning scene and then an evening one. 'Aurora' means the dawn; the suggestion of light on the horizon linking to the album title. Gradually fading in, the pretty composition creates an unsettled and intriguing atmosphere, with sudden modulations and irregular bar lengths. The minor key and Karen's low vocal match the melancholy lyric about sadness, shadows and grey. The final line 'My dreams are songs I play' directs the listener to the songs in a way similar to 'Invocation', 'A Song For You' and 'Sing' on previous albums.

'Only Yesterday' (Richard Carpenter, John Bettis)
Single A-side b/w 'Happy'
Release date: 14 March 1975
Charts: US: 4, UK: 7
With this song, Richard and Bettis deliberately set out to write a hit to follow 'Please Mr Postman'. The arrangement of 'Only Yesterday' bears similarities to

The Ronettes' 1963 hit 'Be My Baby'. These include the opening drum pattern (similar to Hal Blaine's on 'Be My Baby'), the new key in the pre-chorus, and the castanets driving the chorus. Billy Joel took similar inspiration for his track 'Say Goodbye to Hollywood' the following year.

Other notable features include Karen's low Eb in the opening lines, the chiming tubular bells in the chorus, and how the saxophone and guitar solos begin with the same phrase. The key goes up a semitone towards the end, where the single version fades, while the album version fades after the following chorus.

Bettis has stated how he wanted to avoid a replay of the nostalgic ache of 'Yesterday Once More', focusing more on the feeling of being in love in the here and now. All the same, the lyric dwells on the pain of loneliness, citing 'sadness', 'troubles' and 'tears'. The phrases 'the dawn breaking the night' and 'morning light' also link back to the album title.

'Only Yesterday' appeared in March 1975: three months before the album. Though it reached 4 in the US charts, it was their last US top-10 hit. The promotional clip shows the band recording in studio D at A&M, and Karen and Richard walking in the Huntington Botanical Gardens in San Marino, California.

'Desperado' (Glenn Frey, Don Henley)
The Eagles released this poignant ballad in 1973 as the title track of their second album. Despite being one of their best-known songs, they never released it as a single, though Linda Ronstadt recorded a version that year, which helped popularise the song.

Also using a piano and strings arrangement, the Carpenters' version adds further country and western elements such as a lonesome harmonica and the distant wail of pedal-steel guitar. Karen's delivery is tender and intimate, as she appeals to someone who's placed himself beyond everyone's help – not unlike the character later described in 'Solitaire'.

'Please Mr. Postman' (Georgia Dobbins, William Garrett, Freddie Gorman, Brian Holland, Robert Bateman)
Single A-side b/w 'This Masquerade'
Release date: 8 November 1974
Charts: US: 1, UK: 2
The original 1961 release of this song as The Marvelettes' debut single was the first on Motown to reach number 1 on the Hot 100. That group had further hits with 'Beechwood 4-5789' and 'The Hunter Gets Captured by the Game'. The Beatles released their version of 'Please Mr. Postman' on *With The Beatles* in 1963. In July 1974, the Carpenters took a short break from touring, to record their version: released in November, seven months ahead of *Horizon*.

The song revolves around the same four chords, though variety is achieved through the use of backing vocals, tubular bells, castanets, handclaps, guitar and saxophone solos. While the lyric refers to the frustration of a long-distance relationship, the overall effect is buoyant and cheerful. They even filmed a promotional clip on the rides at Disneyland, as if to match the song's fun level, and presumably, Mr. Guder raised no objections this time.

Richard later commented that the single was a regressive step for the band, who by that time should've put their 1960s covers behind them. He admits he had to be reminded to smile in the video, though he must've taken some comfort from the record's phenomenal success. Topping the charts in six countries and going top five in a further four, it became the band's second-biggest international single (after 'Yesterday Once More'). It was voted number 1 on *The Nation's Favourite Carpenters' Song* UK TV program in 2016, though unfortunately, it was their last number one in the US.

'I Can Dream, Can't I' (Irving Kahal, Sammy Fain)
Side one concludes with an affectionate homage to the dance-band music that the duo's parents had grown up with. Richard was also influenced by Harry Nilsson's 1973 standards album: *A Little Touch of Schmilsson in the Night*.

The song had been recorded by Tommy Dorsey and his Orchestra in 1937, Al Bowlly in 1938, The Andrews Sisters in 1949, and Mama Cass in 1969. The music was written by Sammy Fain, known for the musicals *Calamity Jane, Hellzapoppin'*, and songs from *Alice in Wonderland* and *Peter Pan*. Lyricist Irving Kahal wrote the enduring ballad 'I'll Be Seeing You' in 1938.

The orchestral jazz arrangement was by film and TV composer Billy May – bandleader and arranger for Ella Fitzgerald, Frank Sinatra, Bing Crosby and comedian Stan Freberg. May created a smooth accompaniment for Karen's rich, heartfelt vocal, consisting of a full orchestra with jazz instruments and velvety backing vocals. Richard was thrilled to work with one of his musical heroes, and May was asked back for future Carpenters albums, despite having taken this song too slow, in Richard's opinion.

'Solitaire' (Neil Sedaka, Phil Cody)
Single A-side b/w 'Love Me for What I Am'
Release date: 18 July 1975
Charts: US: 17, UK: 32
Side two opens with a love ballad based on a gambling metaphor written by Neil Sedaka with lyricist Phil Cody. Sedaka released his version as an album track in 1972, recorded at 10cc's Strawberry Studios in Stockport, UK. Petula Clark, Tony Christie and The Searchers all recorded earlier versions, though Andy Williams scored the biggest hit with it, taking it to number 4 in the UK in 1973.

In the booklet accompanying the *From the Top* compilation, Richard states that he considered the duo's recording to have captured one of Karen's 'finest performances', though in Lennox and May's book, he conceded that Karen didn't like the song.

Above: From the photo session for the cover of *A Kind Of Hush*, 1976.
(*Ed Caraeff/Alamy*)

Left: The original title and less than promising cover photo for the duo's 1969 debut album *Offering*. (*A&M*)

Right: A new title and a far more promising cover photo for the reissued debut album *Ticket To Ride,* 1970. (*A&M*)

Left: Their successful 1970 sophomore album *Close To You* showcases their first number one. (*A&M*)

Right: The eponymous third album, *Carpenters* (1971), was packaged like a manila envelope, leading to its Beatles-inspired nickname 'The Tan Album'. (*A&M*)

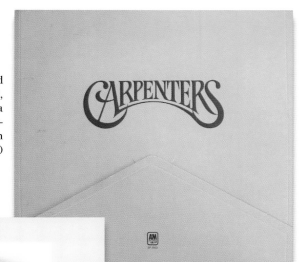

Left: Inner sleeve portrait from *Carpenters* (1971). This photo replaced the plain brown front cover in some countries. (*A&M*)

Right: 1972 brought their fourth album, *A Song For You*, containing six hit singles. (*A&M*)

Left: *Now And Then* (1973) shows the duo in Richard's Ferrari Daytona car, passing the house they shared with their parents in Downey, California. (*A&M*)

Right: *Horizon* (1975). Now a well-established act, the original front cover had just a photo of the pair with no further information. (*A&M*)

Left: The *Horizon* (1975) inner sleeve portrait. (*A&M*)

Right: Their 1976 album *A Kind Of Hush* contains Karen's favourite song: 'I Need To Be In Love'. (*A&M*)

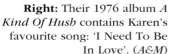

Left: The duo explored a variety of musical styles on their eighth album, *Passage* (1977). (*A&M*)

PASSAGE

Right: Their long-held plans to make a Christmas album became a reality in 1978 with the release of *Christmas Portrait*. (*A&M*)

This page: Karen drums and sings for 'Close To You' and 'We've Only Just Begun' on *The Ed Sullivan Show* in 1970.

This page: From a studio concert broadcast by the BBC in 1971 during the band's first tour of the UK.

Left: A fresh sound for a new decade – *Made In America* (1981). (*A&M*)

Right: The *Made In America* (1981) inner sleeve portrait. (*A&M*)

Left: *Voice Of The Heart* (1983). Karen passed away having recorded two new songs, the remainder being outtakes from 1976 to 1981. (*A&M*)

Right: The inner sleeve of *Voice Of The Heart* – a shot by Annie Leibovitz taken for their *Rolling Stone* feature in 1974. (*A&M*)

Left: Their second Christmas-themed album, *An Old Fashioned Christmas* (1984). (*A&M*)

Right: *If I Were A Carpenter* (1994). An unforeseen but enjoyable tribute album from a range of 1990s alternative rock acts. (*A&M*)

Left: Performing '(They Long To Be) Close To You' at the RAI in Amsterdam, Netherlands for the *Grand Gala Du Disque*, 1974.

Right: 'Close To You' at the RAI in Amsterdam. Guitarist Tony Peluso plays bass for this performance.

Left: Introducing a madcap, Spike Jones-inspired 'Close To You' live at The New London Theatre in 1976. From the specially recorded *The Carpenters: A World Of Music*.

Right: Richard sings the 'two-man band' updated version of 'Piano Picker' at The New London Theatre, 1976.

Left: To promote *Made In America* in Europe, the Carpenters performed 'Touch Me When We're Dancing' on the French TV show *Palmarès 81* in October 1981.

Right: Karen sang her lead vocal live to a backing track for the *Palmarès 81* French TV appearance in 1981.

Left: *Live At The Palladium* (1976) was recorded during their week-long residency at London's Palladium in November 1976 and released the following month. (*A&M*)

Right: *Live At Budokan 1974* is a DVD of the Carpenters' first-ever concert in Japan, launching a fortnight of shows across the country. (*A&M*)

Left: Their first international compilation, *The Singles: 1969-1973* (1973) was also their first number-one album in the US and UK. (*A&M*)

Right: *The Singles: 74-78* (1978). Their second international compilation included ten A-sides and two B-sides but wasn't released in the US. (*A&M*)

Left: *Lovelines* (1989). A cohesive compilation featuring band outtakes and the first release of four tracks recorded for Karen's solo album. (*A&M*)

Right: *From The Top* (1991). This box set of rarities and remixes was reissued as *The Essential Collection: 1965-1997* (2002) with a revised song selection. (*A&M*)

Left: The compilation *As Time Goes By* (2001) combined studio outtakes with TV appearances and early demos dating back to 1967. (*A&M*)

Right: *Time* (1987). Richard's first solo album, featuring new material and lead vocals from Richard, Dusty Springfield, Dionne Warwick and newcomer Scott Grimes. (*A&M*)

Left: *Karen Carpenter* (1996) is Karen's only solo album, recorded in New York during 1979 and 1980 and posthumously released in 1996. (*A&M*)

Right: *Richard Carpenter: Pianist, Arranger, Composer, Conductor* (1998). Richard's second solo album revisits Carpenters' classics with orchestra, band and choir. (*A&M*)

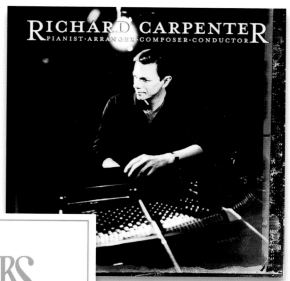

Left: *Carpenters With The Royal Philharmonic Orchestra* (2018). Richard adds new orchestral parts to existing Carpenters recordings at Abbey Road Studios in London. (*A&M*)

Right: *Richard Carpenter's Piano Songbook* (2023). Richard's third solo album features solo piano interpretations of the Carpenters' catalogue. (*Decca*)

Left: Sheet music booklet for *Top Of The World*. (*Rondor Music Ltd, from the author's collection*)

Right: *Carpenters Song Book*. 1970s Japanese publication with songs from the first five albums. (*Shinko Music, from the author's collection*)

The arrangement follows the usual Carpenters pattern for slow songs – a quiet opening verse of piano and voice before the entry of other instruments, building to a fuller texture in the chorus. Of note is how the slide guitar plays rising figures in the second verse, illustrating the phrases 'a little hope' and 'goes up in smoke'. The song reaches a climactic halt on the final chorus, whereafter, the melody is passed from piano to oboe to strings. The single mix included additional lead guitar and organ.

No Carpenters single reached the US top 10 again, though they would continue to achieve top ten placings on the Easy Listening chart.

'Happy' (Tony Peluso, Diane Rubin, John Bettis)
For the only upbeat song on side two, John Bettis collaborated with guitarist Tony Peluso and singer Diane Rubin.

Karen's vocal is cheerful and well-suited to the song title. The music is based on a picked pattern played on acoustic guitar and phased electric guitar. Richard plays an Arp Odyssey synthesizer, manufactured in 1972 in competition with Moog's Minimoog. He uses the synth in different ways, creating a staccato pattern, and ending with a series of higher and higher-pitched portamento notes to convey a sense of happiness.

The track was chosen as the 'Only Yesterday' B-side, though many fans felt that 'Happy' could've been a hit single in its own right. Japanese fans voted for its inclusion on the 2000 compilation *By Request*.

'(I'm Caught Between) Goodbye And I Love You' (Richard Carpenter, John Bettis)
John Bettis has stated that he wanted to capture the struggle that he and the duo faced in sustaining romantic relationships, especially in Richard and Karen's case, due to the time spent out on the road and in the studio. The lyric depicts one last attempt to save a relationship, and the band offers sympathetic backing. The chorus' final line recalls the classic 1931 jazz standard 'Between the Devil and the Deep Blue Sea': recorded by Cab Calloway, Ella Fitzgerald, Perry Como and others.

'Love Me For What I Am' (Palma Pascale, John Bettis)
With a similar theme to the prior song, Bettis teamed up with Contemporary Christian writer Palma Pascale on this exacting audit of a relationship. Karen adopts a confidential tone in the verses, becoming strident and assertive in the choruses. The song enters power-ballad territory with Tony Peluso's fuzz guitar solo, giving the album a dramatic penultimate number.

'Eventide' (Richard Carpenter, John Bettis)
'Eventide' bookends the album with the same instrumental backing track as the opener 'Aurora'. The mysterious piano fade-in returns. It previously represented the rising sun, but now suggests the evening and slow drawing in of night.

Like that of 'Aurora', the lyric employs poetic imagery, with the sunset described as a 'velvet rose'. Karen sings of 'barren skies' and weariness, though the final image of 'candles burning by the sea' conjures a Californian idyll of evening beach parties or a romantic midnight liaison. The final piano chord slowly fades, leaving a lingering impression of the album's pensive mood.

The title is linked to the 19th-century hymn 'Abide with Me', the lyric of which includes the line 'Fast falls the eventide'. Fittingly, this hymn's lyrics are most often sung to the tune known as 'Eventide'. The hymn addresses themes of death as the dark evening arrives at the end of the day, or at the end of one's life.

Related Tracks
'Trying To Get The Feeling Again' (David Pomeranz)
Single A-side b/w 'Sing', '(They Long To Be) Close To You'
Release date: 1994
Charts: UK: 44

Songwriter David Pomeranz was a solo artist, opening for Billy Joel, Rod Stewart, Three Dog Night, and the Carpenters in the mid-1970s. His songs have been recorded by Bette Midler, Phoebe Snow and Cliff Richard, and Pomeranz has also written for Broadway, film and TV.

Warner Bros. Music commissioned Pomeranz to write this especially for the Carpenters. The recording was originally planned for *Horizon,* but was left unfinished due to a predominance of ballads on the album. So the track releases include Karen's guide vocal, recorded in one take and intended for later replacement. Keen listeners will catch the sound of the lyric sheet being turned over at the end of the first chorus.

Pomeranz based the lyric on his own troubled marriage. After submitting the demo to the Carpenters, he didn't hear back at first. Rewriting the lyric, he sent a revised demo to Bette Midler, who passed it on to her producer Barry Manilow. Midler didn't record it, and before Manilow recorded his version, Pomeranz had revised the lyrics a second time. Karen's recording includes the first version of the lyric, Manilow's the second, and Pomeranz's the third, which he released on his 1975 album *It's in Every One of Us*. Manilow had the biggest success with the song, taking it to number 10 in 1975. Gene Pitney, flautist Hubert Laws and singer Dee Dee Sharp Gamble all released versions not long after.

The Carpenters' recording was presumed lost before engineer Roger Young discovered it in 1991 on the same multitrack tape as 'Only Yesterday'. The arrangement includes drums from Jim Gordon, and a stirring guitar solo from Tony Peluso, though the Beatles-esque string parts were added in 1994 when the track was being prepared for the compilation *Interpretations: A 25th Anniversary Celebration*. This version was issued as a single in the UK. The track then underwent further remixing in 1995, to eliminate Karen's vocal mouth sounds, and it was then included on the US issue of *Interpretations*.

'Good Friends Are For Keeps' (Joe Silberman)

This one-minute radio advertisement was recorded for the Ma Bell telephone company (otherwise known as AT&T) in Studio D in 1975. Karen provides vocals and drums, Richard vocals and keyboards, with Tony Peluso on guitar and bass. The ad was remixed in 1990 for the *From the Top* and *The Essential Collection: 1965-1997* compilations.

A Kind Of Hush (1976)

Personnel:
Karen Carpenter: vocals, vibraphone
Richard Carpenter: vocals, keyboards, vibraphone, orchestrator, arranger
Joe Osborn: bass
Tony Peluso: guitar
Bob Messenger: flute, tenor saxophone and cheek pop on 'Goofus'
Doug Strawn: whistle on 'Can't Smile Without You'
Jim Horn: baritone sax
Earle Dumler: oboe, English horn
Tom Scott: clarinet, flute
David Shostac: flute
Wes Jacobs: tuba
Jim Gordon, Cubby O'Brien: drums
Gayle Levant, Dorothy Remsen: harp
The MOR Chorale: backing vocals
Special thanks to Ron Gorow, Ed Sulzer and John Bettis
Produced by Richard Carpenter
Associate Producer: Karen Carpenter
Engineered by Ray Gerhardt and Dave Iveland
Recorded at A&M Records, Hollywood, California
Release date: 11 June 1976
Label: A&M
Charts: US: 33 UK: 3
Running Time 34:00

With recording for *Horizon* completed, the band were on the road from April to August 1975. Sadly, Karen was still pursuing a strict diet and was down to 86 lbs. Proud of her new figure, she bought clothes to show it off. Making her stage entrances in backless dresses, audiences gasped at the sight of her bony shoulders and visible rib cage. Further misfortune arrived in July when Neil Sedaka joined the tour as support act. Sedaka had enjoyed a run of hits as a pop star and songwriter in the early 1960s, his career having stalled for the rest of that decade. His slow return to fame included recording in the UK at Strawberry Studios with 10cc as his backing group, while his new songs were being covered by the likes of Abba, The 5th Dimension, Lou Christie and Helen Reddy. Finally, in February 1975, Sedaka reached number one with the joyful 'Laughter in the Rain'. Sharing the same management as the Carpenters, he joined the tour as opening act, promoting his new album *Sedaka's Back*. According to press accounts, Sedaka's lively, hit-filled set had audiences on their feet, while the Carpenters' performances achieved only polite applause – that is until Sedaka returned to the stage during the Carpenters' encores to sing golden oldies with them, which brought the audiences back to life.

By the time they began a fortnight's residency at Las Vegas' Riviera Hotel, Sedaka was clearly enjoying the spotlight so much that Richard would come onstage to find broken piano keys. The final straw came when Sedaka also broke stage protocol by introducing celebrity audience members Dick Clark and Tom Jones: a gesture traditionally reserved for the headline act. Richard was furious, and the next day, Sedaka was sacked. To save face, he swiftly called a press conference to contend that he'd been fired for being too strong an opening act, bringing further embarrassment to the Carpenters.

Karen – already exhausted from the tour – was deeply upset by the incident, and suffered something of a nervous collapse, checking into the Cedars-Sinai Medical Center. The band's upcoming tours of Japan and Europe had to be cancelled, bringing a huge financial loss. Richard visited the countries in person, holding press conferences to apologise and explain how their heavy schedule had led to a decline in Karen's health. In the meantime, Karen's mother was nursing her at home, and Karen was sleeping 14-16 hours a day. As she recovered, her weight increased to a more healthy 104 lbs.

A further outcome of the Sedaka debacle had been that both artists had dropped their mutual manager, Sherwin Bash. In January 1976, the Carpenters signed with Jerry Weintraub: former manager for Frank Sinatra, Elvis Presley and Judy Garland. Weintraub vowed to reduce their touring and allow more time for recording. That same month, they also signed a new contract with A&M.

Sessions for their seventh album, *A Kind Of Hush,* commenced in December 1975 at A&M Studio D. Karen didn't play drums on this or any subsequent Carpenters studio album; drumming duties for this album split between Jim Gordon and Cubby O'Brien. Curiously, the first song recorded was Neil Sedaka's 'Breaking Up is Hard to Do', as if to bury the hatchet. Recording continued until mid-March when the band flew to Japan for four weeks of concerts. They returned to the studio in April, and the album was released in June.

The front cover shows them smiling from a window, while the back cover has a view of Earth against an evening sunset, presumably illustrating the album's opening line, 'There's a kind of hush all over the world tonight'. The album eventually achieved gold status, though it fell behind the last six albums, which had all gone platinum or multi-platinum.

The first two singles – 'There's A Kind Of Hush (All Over The World)' and 'I Need to Be in Love' – both reached the top 30, though the third – 'Goofus' – was less successful and stalled outside the top 50. Richard considered 'One More Time' and 'Sandy' to be among the album's best tracks, and while he acknowledged the album's overall high-quality production and performances, he nevertheless regrets the inclusion of two more 1960s oldies and the even older 'Goofus' from the 1930s. If the band were to stay relevant, future albums were going to need a new approach.

'There's A Kind Of Hush (All Over The World)' (Les Reed, Geoff Stephens)

Single A-side b/w '(I'm Caught Between) Goodbye and I Love You'
Release date: 7 February 1976
Charts: US: 12, UK: 22

The album is bookended with two 1960s covers. The title song originally reached number 4 in 1967, as performed by British Invasion band Herman's Hermits, who enjoyed several US hit singles in the 1960s, including 'I'm into Something Good' and 'No Milk Today'.

Songwriter Les Reed had previously scored hits with The Fortunes and Tom Jones. Geoff Stephens had managed the UK artist Donovan, and had also formed The New Vaudeville Band, who made the first recording of 'There's A Kind Of Hush'. Other artists to release the song in the 1960s included Engelbert Humperdinck, Trini Lopez and Jim Nabors. Richard was reminded of the song when looking through a book of 1960s chart listings, and remembered he and Karen being fans of it.

The Carpenters' version starts with Tony Peluso's guitar copying the wordless melody sung by Hermits' singer Peter Noone in the middle of their version. Karen emphasises the 'shh' of 'hush' in imitation of Noone, while Richard creates a chirping sound with the ARP synthesizer (partially removed in the 1985 remix). The saxophone and guitar solos are played by Bob Messenger and Tony Peluso, respectively, while castanets add a Spanish rhythm that's doubled on muted guitar strings.

A promotional clip shot during the 1976 spring Japan tour shows the band miming to the song onstage.

'You' (Randy Edelman)

Single A-side b/w 'I Have You' (Philippines)

'You' was the third Randy Edelman song the duo covered. Like the prior two, the lyric refers to making music: 'You are the crowd that sits quiet listening to me' and 'Just like the old love song goes'. The recording was slightly sped-up, and this version was also used for two 1990s compilations. The track was restored to its original speed for the 1998 CD remaster.

'Sandy' (Richard Carpenter, John Bettis)

The first of the album's three Carpenter/Bettis collaborations was named for the band's on-the-road hairdresser, Sandy Holland. The lyric makes a nod to 'Rainy Days And Mondays' on the line 'You know how rainy weather gets me down when I'm alone'. The arrangement has a dreamy quality, while the Fender Rhodes piano tremolo creates a floating sensation. Add to this a key centre that shifts four times, and the overall effect is quite spellbinding. A flute solo leads to the outro, which alternates between two chords. Richard returned to this two-chord sequence in his 1987 solo song 'Time'.

'Sandy' has become something of a fan favourite, appearing on several compilations, including *Treasures* and *Sweet Memories*.

'Goofus' (Wayne King, William Harold, Gus Kahn)
Single A-side b/w 'Boat to Sail'
Release date: 11 August 1976
Charts: US: 56, UK: -
The first recording of the comic tune 'Goofus' appeared in 1931, with lyrics by Gus Kahn, who wrote the classics 'It Had to Be You', 'My Baby Just Cares for Me', 'Dream a Little Dream of Me' and 'Love Me or Leave Me'. His collaborators were bandleader Wayne King and violinist William Harold from Wayne King's orchestra. Over the years, the lighthearted song has been a popular choice for country and trad-jazz artists, jug bands and big bands. The duo no doubt heard Les Paul's 1950 recording when they were growing up. Other artists to cover the song included Chet Atkins, Lawrence Welk, and comedian Phil Harris: the voice of Baloo the Bear in Disney's *The Jungle Book*.

The jocular lyric pokes fun at a rustic hick and his idiosyncratic approach to playing music. My sheet music copy has the instruction 'Tempo di Rube'.

The Carpenters give the vintage song an update with a funky drum rhythm played by their touring drummer, Cubby O'Brien. In keeping with the theme, handclaps appear on offbeats to ensure there is something a little bit off about the track. Bob Messenger plays some raucous rock-and-roll saxophone, and contributed the cheek pop heard on the outro. Karen delivers the vocal with faux innocence, while tuba player Wes Jacobs returns to play an intentionally basic part. Richard's honky-tonk piano and Tony Peluso's picking solo lend a country air. Further mischief comes in the last line which repeats as if the record player needle is jumping.

The track was the album's third single at Karen's request, but was their lowest chart placing since their 1969 debut single, 'Ticket To Ride'. Richard regrets the release of 'Goofus' as a single, while fans remain divided over track.

'Can't Smile Without You' (Chris Arnold, David Martin, Geoff Morrow)
The first recording of this era-defining 1970s song was released by its composer David Martin in 1975, but was not a hit. The British writing trio had penned songs for artists like Elvis Presley, Cass Elliot and Jack Jones since the 1960s, and also recorded together as the band Butterscotch. The Carpenters were second to release the song, followed by Engelbert Humperdinck and UK duo Peters and Lee, before Barry Manilow issued the song's best-known recording in 1978.

The Carpenters' version gradually grows from voice and electric piano to include strings, vibraphone, flugelhorn and harp, with a brief, big-band-style trumpet break in the middle. But all of this is as nothing to the bombastic version Manilow took to number 3 in the charts. Where Martin's and the

Carpenters' versions include two key changes, Manilow's version changes three times, climaxing with a high-kicking finale.

For the song's release on the B-side of 'Calling Occupants Of Interplanetary Craft' in 1977, Richard and Karen re-recorded the opening verse at a faster speed, adding clarinet and flute to join the trumpets on the instrumental break. Karen also sang new words in the opening chorus, changing 'and I can't walk, I'm finding it hard even to talk' to 'and I can't sleep, I don't even talk to people I meet'. Manilow later changed these lines to 'and I can't sing, I'm finding it hard to do anything', but was happy to keep the whistling part heard at the end of the Carpenters' version, performing it in the introduction of his recording.

'I Need To Be In Love' (Richard Carpenter, John Bettis, Albert Hammond)
Single A-side b/w 'Sandy'
Release date: 21 May 1976
Charts: US: 25, UK: 36
Side two begins with the album's second single – a Carpenter/Bettis original begun as an idea by British-born songwriter Albert Hammond. His hits to this point included 'The Air That I Breathe', 'It Never Rains in Southern California' and '99 Miles from L.A.'. He thought of the title and opening melody lines while he and Bettis were working on songs in England, and it was later completed by Bettis and Richard.

The lyric is especially poignant, including the opening image '...wide awake at 4 am without a friend in sight'. Randy Schmidt's biography quotes an interview where Bettis described the lyric as coming 'out of my heart straight to Karen's'. Correspondingly, Karen was greatly taken by the song, calling it her favourite Carpenters song, and delivering an arresting performance.

All were convinced it would become a hit, and it was released just ahead of the album. The track received some airplay, but took two months to reach the top 30, peaking at a respectable 25. But this fell short of the band's expectations, being their first single in six years to not reach the top 20. Richard thinks the tune might've been a little too sophisticated to be a single, requiring more than just one listen to make a connection with the listener.

Reaching 62 in Japan, the song was given a second life there in 1995 when it was used as the closing theme to Japanese TV drama *Miseinen*. Paired with 'Top Of The World' (the programme's opening theme), it reached number 5, becoming one of the band's most recognised songs in Japan.

While the single removed the piano introduction, compilations from 1990 onwards used the full-length track in a new remixed by Richard.

'One More Time' (Lewis Anderson)
The duo first heard this fragile ballad when songwriter Anderson appeared as their opening act. Anderson had also placed songs with Kenny Rogers, America and The Neville Brothers.

In the lyric, the narrator takes an imaginary journey to visit friends and family in Louisiana: the US state in which Anderson grew up.

Richard's piano follows a free tempo, tracing mysterious chords and leaving reflective pauses while Karen interprets the lyric with sensitivity, as if telling her own story. One of the album's more subtle selections, it certainly rewards repeated listening. Seals and Crofts – on their 1978 album *Takin' It Easy* – recorded a soft-rocking version which included a Beach Boys-esque *a cappella* introduction.

'Boat To Sail' (Jackie DeShannon)

This writer of this laid-back number was best known for her songs for Brenda Lee, The Byrds, and The Searchers, who had a 1964 hit with DeShannon's 'When You Walk in the Room'. She released her own version of the song on her 1975 album *New Arrangement*, which included songs written with John Bettis, and also 'Bette Davis Eyes': a 1981 hit for Kim Carnes.

The lyric describes the perfect escape from everyday life, sailing boats in the Caribbean. Beach Boy Brian Wilson is referred to, along with his song 'Don't Worry Baby'. Following this, the backing vocals add Beach Boys-style phrases. At the end, Karen credits the writer with the affectionate message 'DeShannon's back'. DeShannon married singer-songwriter Randy Edelman on 3 June 1976: eight days before the *A Kind Of Hush* album came out.

'I Have You' (Richard Carpenter, John Bettis)

This easy-listening ballad is the album's third Carpenter/Bettis song. Strings dominate, and Karen's harmonies are somewhat reminiscent of Abba. Incidentally, the Carpenters actually began recording a version of Abba's 'Thank You for the Music' in 1978 but subsequently decided they could add nothing new to the Abba original.

'I Have You' was a 1978 single in Mexico, with 'Sweet, Sweet Smile' on the B-side.

'Breaking Up Is Hard To Do' (Neil Sedaka, Howard Greenfield)

Single A-side b/w 'I Have You' (Japan)
Release date: 1976
Charts: Japan: 71

A lively – though puzzling – way to end the record just after they'd very publicly broken up with Sedaka, this cover of his 1962 song is the album's other 1960s bookend. Sedaka himself revisited the song as a ballad on his 1975 album *The Hungry Years*. Richard actually contributed the string arrangement for Sedaka's new recording, which might've been another reason it was on Richard's mind when choosing songs for this album.

The Carpenters' version was assembled over five separate sessions between December 1975 and April 1976. Karen sings with herself over a cha-cha rhythm, using the same combination of castanet and muted guitar heard on

73

'There's A Kind Of Hush'. Joe Osborn's bass part is echoed by Jim Horn's baritone saxophone, while Bob Messenger delivers a tenor saxophone solo to cowbell accompaniment. The key then moves up a half-step for the final verse and outro with boisterous chants of 'hard to do'. The ending's background dialogue includes Doug Strawn impersonating Inspector Clouseau from the *Pink Panther* films, saying the line 'Try to do something about your filthy monkey'.

Related Tracks
'Medley: Superstar/Rainy Days And Mondays' (Leon Russell/Bonnie Bramlett, Paul Williams/Roger Nichols)

Though the duo's TV series *Make Your Own Kind of Music* had aired back in 1971, they were so unhappy with the results that they were now still against the idea of starring in their own TV show. But it had been a while since their last top-10 single, and they were no doubt thinking of this when their new manager, Jerry Weintraub asked them to give the format another go. The new show was rehearsed and taped in September and early October, before the duo headed out on a tour of the US and Europe. *The Carpenters' Very First TV Special* was broadcast in December 1976, and was rated the sixth most popular show that week. This success encouraged the duo to make a further four specials for ABC between 1977 and 1980.

The TV special featured songs and sketches with special guests Victor Borge and John Denver, and a brief filmed cameo from Olivia Newton John. The comic routines included 'These Are the Jokes, Folks': a *bossa nova* number over which the duo sang their way through a string of old gags, and a version of 'Close To You' performed by Richard and the band in the madcap style of Spike Jones and His City Slickers. The straight routines included John Denver and Karen duetting on a medley of Robert Burns' 'Comin' Thro' the Rye' and The Beach Boys' 'Good Vibrations'. Karen also gave an energetic performance of her drum solo over Gershwin tunes from their live show, using special televisual effects to duet with herself on two drum kits. At the start and end of the show, Richard conducted an orchestra playing a disco version of 'We've Only Just Begun', and the same arrangement featured on all of their subsequent TV specials.

Another sequence featured Karen singing a medley of 'Superstar' and 'Rainy Days And Mondays'. This recording was reworked for the 2001 Japanese rarities compilation *As Time Goes B*y. Working from mono recordings, Richard re-recorded the piano and drums in stereo, adding new parts from Joe Osborn on bass, Tommy Morgan on harmonica, and an expanded orchestra.

'Hits Medley '76'

The TV special finale was an eight-minute medley featuring seven of the duo's hits spanning the era 1969-1975. They're shown performing in a recording studio with an orchestra and their touring band, all dressed in matching red outfits. The medley included sections from 'Sing', 'Close To You', 'For All We Know', 'Ticket To Ride', 'Only Yesterday', 'I Won't Last a Day Without You' and 'Goodbye To Love'. Karen sang the parts live to pre-recorded backing. Richard organised for the original mono piano and drums to be re-recorded in stereo for the medley's inclusion on the *As Time Goes By* compilation.

Passage (1977)

Personnel:
Karen Carpenter: vocals
Richard Carpenter: vocals, keyboards (2, 3, 6, 7, 8), orchestrator, arranger
Joe Osborn: bass
Tony Peluso: guitar
Pete Jolly: piano (1)
Larry Muhoberac: electric piano (1)
Ron Tutt: drums (1, 3, 5, 8)
Wally Snow, Jerry Steinholtz: percussion (1)
Tommy Vig: percussion (1, 7)
Gene Perling: vocal arrangement (1)
Tom Scott: tenor saxophone, alto flute
Ed Green: drums (2, 6, 7)
Ray Parker: guitar (2)
Karen and Richard Carpenter, Julia Tillman, Carlena Williams, Maxine Willard:
backing vocals (2)
Earle Dumler: oboe
Gayle Levant: harp
Overbudget (Los Angeles) Philharmonic – Peter Knight: conductor (3, 4, 8) and
orchestrator (3, 4, 8)
Gregg Smith Singers: backing vocals with Gregg Smith as conductor (3, 4, 8)
Dennis Heath: announcer (4)
William Feuerstein: peron (4)
Jonathan Marks: che (4)
Bobby Bruce: fiddle (5)
Larry McNealy: banjo (5)
Tom Hensley: tack piano (5, 7)
Lee Ritenour, Jay Graydon: acoustic guitar (6)
Jay Dee Maness: pedal steel guitar (6)
Leon Russell: piano (7)
Vince Charles: steel drums (7)
David Luell and Kurt McGettrick: baritone saxophone (7)
Jackie Kelso: tenor saxophone (7)
King Erisson: conga (7)
Special thanks to Ron Gorow, Ed Sulzer and John Bettis
Produced by Richard Carpenter
Associate Producer: Karen Carpenter
Engineered by Ray Gerhardt, Roger Young and Dave Iveland
Recorded at A&M Records, Hollywood, California
Release date: 23 September 1977
Label: A&M
Charts: US: 49, UK: 12
Running Time 39:39

Following the disappointing sales of *A Kind Of Hush*, Karen and Richard went to A&M's Jerry Moss for advice, and he suggested bringing in an outside producer. The idea appealed to Richard, but each producer they approached turned them down. In the end, Richard resumed his usual production role, but he also knew it was time to take the band in a new direction. The question was, what should that new direction be?

Change was certainly in the air. Established artists like Elton John, Abba and – most notably – the Bee Gees, were embracing disco. A&M also had an eye on the emerging new-wave scene. Having failed to tame the Sex Pistols, the label was to have greater success with new acts like The Police, Squeeze and Joe Jackson.

Passage – the Carpenters' eighth album – saw the band seemingly move in all directions at once in the search for a new sound, juxtaposing progressive rock, calypso, country and more. Puzzled listeners could seek help from the album sleeve notes (written by journalists Tom Nolan and Digby Diehl), but, clearly, much more was needed when the album reached only 49 in the US, where it didn't even qualify for silver sales. Luckily, overseas fans were more adventurous, with *Passage* reaching seven in Japan, and 12 in the UK, where it went gold.

The recording sessions ran from March to May 1977, with several tracks cut live as a band rather than recording parts separately. The ultimate example of this came on 24 May when over 100 orchestra players and 50 choir members came in to record 'On the Balcony of the Casa Rosada/Don't Cry for Me Argentina' (from the musical *Evita*). Journalists were invited to watch the session take place on the A&M soundstage, while Karen sang from a vocal booth in Studio D. The initial session for 'Calling Occupants Of Interplanetary Craft' also took place that day, but the trumpet parts were found to have leaked onto other instrument tracks, which necessitated further recording later that week.

As per their last record, Karen didn't play any drums. But more surprising was the arrival of four players to either supplement or replace Richard on keyboards. *Passage* was also the first Carpenters album to not have a Carpenter/Bettis composition. In truth, Richard's reduced involvement was mostly due to his escalating intake of Quaaludes: the sedative he'd first used as a sleeping pill on tour in 1971. His addiction had worsened over the past few years, and it was a further two years before he was finally able to quit.

The album cover art represented another break with the past, opting for a colourful illustration of musical notes flying off the page, rather than having a photo of the duo or focusing on their logo. It was designed by Lou Beach (who previously designed artwork for fusion band Weather Report), and was replicated in reverse on the back cover, making the musical notes appear to land back on the page. The illustration included an artistic rendering of the band name in loose brush strokes rather than their more familiar logo, although this could be found at the bottom of the back cover, albeit in a discrete smaller size.

Despite the changes, the album had the same high standard of musicianship and production, and – if nothing else – proved the duo's versatility. Once again, the singles were only modest successes, though 'Calling Occupants Of Interplanetary Craft' enjoyed top-10 success abroad. Over time, Richard came to regard the album as too great a departure from their established sound, though their next release would be a departure of a different kind.

'B'wana She No Home' (Michael Franks)
Idiosyncratic singer-songwriter Michael Franks had scored a modest top 50 hit in 1976 with his whimsical song 'Popsicle Toes', covered shortly afterwards by The Manhattan Transfer. In January 1977, Franks released his Latin-inspired album *Sleeping Gypsy,* which included 'B'wana-He No Home'.

Three months later, the duo went into A&M's Studio D to record their version, which captured the spirit of Franks' original, fashioning the same groove at roughly the same tempo. New additions include a key change to suit Karen's voice, with backing vocals and saxophones to thicken the sound. Drummer Ron Scott and two percussionists created the restless rhythm, while Joe Osborn added a snaky bass line. Guitarist Tony Peluso played decorative lead licks with a spacey phasing effect, while Tom Scott played flute and saxophone solos between the verses. Scott, whose extensive credits include working with Joni Mitchell, Paul Williams and three members of The Beatles, had previously appeared on *Now And Then* and *A Kind Of Hush*. Pianist Pete Jolly reappeared from the *Horizon* album to supply the insistent riff and busy solo that starts from 4:15. Richard didn't play on the track – the Fender Rhodes accompaniment provided by Larry Muhoberac.

The wry and humorous lyric is a fictional account of a time when Franks left his home in the care of singer/guitarist Dan Hicks. Hicks had been a member of 1960s psychedelic group The Charlatans, who were known to have taken LSD while performing live from as early as 1965. He later formed the band Dan Hicks and His Hot Licks, but by the late-1970s had acquired a reputation for difficult behaviour on account of his drug and alcohol addictions – all of which no doubt explains why the character in the song likes 'to be here alone', and especially why the maid is instructed to 'peel your eyes for the heat': or in other words, keep an eye out for the police.

The lyric's dry humour has not aged entirely well, and the tone the speaker uses towards the Ecuadorian maid may make some listeners uncomfortable. The term 'B'wana', meaning 'boss' or 'master', derives from Swahili rather than the maid's native Spanish, but presumably was the right fit for the chorus.

This was certainly not the last unfamiliar role Karen was to play on this album. While she delivered the vocal in a conversational tone, the melody required her to use almost the full scope of her vocal range, rising to a high B in the choruses and dropping to an Eb in the verses.

'All You Get From Love Is A Love Song' (Steve Eaton)

Single A-side b/w 'I Have You'
Release date: 2 May 1977
Charts: US: 35, UK: 54

Songwriter Steve Eaton released the original slightly slower version of
this song in 1974, but the Carpenters' version more closely resembles The
Righteous Brothers' 1975 recording. While the new arrangement is a little
faster and in a different key, the two recordings share some of the same
musicians: Ed Greene on drums, and Tom Scott on saxophone – who even
recycles lines from his original solo. Karen is joined by the same backing
singers from the Steve Eaton recording: Maxine Willard, Julia Tillman and
Carlena Williams (a former Ikette with Ike and Tina Turner).

Richard plays electric and acoustic piano parts, Tony Peluso is on guitar
and further guitar parts are by Ray Parker Jnr. (whose band Raydio would
score a hit with 'Jack and Jill' later the same year ahead of his greater success
with the 'Ghostbusters' theme in 1984). The song also includes elements that
are also associated with disco, such as the congas and guiro, trumpet stabs
and flute harmonies.

In contrast to the prior song, Karen's vocal delivery is smooth and relaxed.
The chorus lyric links being in love with songwriting in a manner similar to
that of 'A Song For You' and 'I Can't Make Music'. The song has a breezy
charm, and Karen had felt certain it would make the perfect lead single ahead
of the new album. While it unquestionably performed better than their last
single, 'Goofus', it only reached a disappointing 35 in the US. A promo film
was shot in Studio D at A&M, with saxophonist Bob Messenger standing in
for Tom Scott on saxophone.

'I Just Fall In Love Again' (Steve Dorff, Larry Herbstritt, Harry Lloyd, Gloria Sklerov)

An engaging and memorable ballad with lush orchestration, this is closer
to the Carpenters' sound of previous albums, albeit without their trademark
vocal harmonies. Richard first heard this song on a demo sent by his friend,
songwriter Stephen Dorff, and Richard knew it would be perfect for Karen's
voice. Dorff and Herbstritt have each had songs recorded by Dionne Warwick,
Melissa Manchester and Cher, while Sklerov and Lloyd's songs have been
recorded by Frank Sinatra, Peggy Lee and Nana Mouskouri. Dorff composed
the theme tune for the sitcom *Growing Pains* with John Bettis in the 1980s.

The arrangement begins softly with Fender Rhodes and oboe, but Karen's
voice is soon soaring high to convey the feeling of repeatedly falling in love
with the same person. A tinkling glockenspiel appears when Karen sings
the word 'magic', and a surge of strings accompanies her reverie of being
transported to Heaven and the stars.

The song's key briefly dips as Tony Peluso begins his power-ballad-style
guitar solo, returning to the original key in the second half of the solo, then

stepping up by a tone for the final rousing chorus with The Gregg Smith Singers.

The orchestration was by British conductor Peter Knight, who flew to L.A. from the UK to work on this and two other tracks on the album. Knight had previously arranged the Moody Blues' psychedelic 1967 album *Days of Future Passed,* conducting the London Festival Orchestra on a conceptual suite that climaxed with the hit 'Nights in White Satin'. On *Passage,* he conducted the Los Angeles Philharmonic Orchestra, who were billed as the 'Overbudget Philharmonic' for contractual reasons.

Though Richard wanted the song released as a single, its running time of four minutes was considered too long for radio. The song became a hit for Anne Murray two years later, going to number one on the country charts and 12 on the *Billboard* Hot 100.

'On The Balcony Of The Casa Rosada'/'Don't Cry For Me Argentina' (Andrew Lloyd Webber, Tim Rice)

Based on the true story of Argentina's president Juan Peron and his wife Eva, Andrew Lloyd Webber and Tim Rice's 1976 musical *Evita* was released first as an album before being adapted for the stage, just as their earlier success *Jesus Christ Superstar* had been. Julie Covington sang the part of Eva on the original recording, taking 'Don't Cry for Me Argentina' to number one in the UK in February 1977, although Elaine Paige made the role her own in the West End. The musical was less well-known in the States before its Broadway opening in 1979, with Patti Lu Pone in the title role.

The Carpenters recording begins with the noise of a great crowd as an announcer introduces the newly elected Juan Peron, who then addresses the crowd from the balcony of his pink palace the Casa Rosada, with critical commentary from Argentine revolutionary Che Guevara. Peron's part is performed by baritone William Feuerstein, and Guevara by the tenor Jonathan Marks.

The musical setting for this scene is tense and unsettled, featuring atonal harmony and irregular rhythms to imply trouble ahead. Building to a dramatic climax, the tension dissolves as 'Don't Cry for Me Argentina' begins, with its soothing strings and gentle bolero rhythm. In this song, Eva Peron – a former radio and TV personality – appeals to the public to accept her in her new role as the country's First Lady.

Though out of keeping with earlier Carpenters recordings, it's worth noting that Petula Clark and Olivia Newton-John had both released versions of the song before the release of *Passage*. On the official Carpenters' website, Richard stated the following:

This song was submitted to us by the publisher, and I immediately felt it was perfect for Karen, though now I feel differently, as I believe the song doesn't linger long enough in a lower register: a great area for Karen's voice.

That may be so, but Karen still turns in a convincing performance in this dramatic role, demonstrating once again her versatility as an interpreter of diverse styles. She can also be heard singing with herself, most noticeably in the opening verses.

Peter Knight arranged and conducted the 100-piece orchestra, joined on the A&M soundstage by a 50-strong choir conducted by Gregg Smith. The sound was wired into Studio D, where Karen recorded her parts from the vocal booth.

According to Coleman's biography of the band, Jerry Moss of A&M had reservations about including the song on the album, considering it to be a 'socialist anthem' and fearing it would be interpreted as a political statement. While the release went ahead in the US, the song was initially left off the album's Argentinian version. 'Don't Cry for Me Argentina' was issued as a single in the US and Canada with 'Calling Occupants...' on the B-side, but wasn't a hit. Karen also sang a Spanish language version, 'No Llores Por Mí Argentina', which was issued in Mexico in 1979.

For the 1996 movie adaptation of *Evita*, the part of Eva Peron went to Madonna – a self-professed Carpenters fan who has stated that her 1993 single 'Rain' is a tribute to Karen. John Bettis co-wrote Madonna's 1985 hit 'Crazy for You'.

'Sweet, Sweet Smile' (Juice Newton, Otha Young)
Single A-side b/w 'I Have You'
Release date: 20 January 1978
Charts: US: 44, UK: 40

In sharp contrast to the Lloyd Webber songs, side two begins with some good-time country pop. Featuring their trademark harmony vocals, 'Sweet, Sweet Smile' is closer to a conventional Carpenters song, though Richard's only musical contribution was as backing vocalist.

Karen brings plenty of energy, accompanied by Bobby Bruce on fiddle, Larry McNealy on banjo and Tom Hensley on tack piano. Tony Peluso adds country licks and a guitar solo while drums come courtesy of industry veteran Ron Tutt, who'd played with Elvis Presley, Emmylou Harris, and on two of Billy Joel's early albums.

Juice Newton – best known for her hit version of 'Angel of the Morning' – wrote 'Sweet, Sweet Smile' with her bandleader Otha Young. Newton originally intended to record the song herself, but her label, Capitol, turned it down. Karen heard a demo of the song through Newton's manager and recommended it to Richard, who agreed it could be a hit. Released as the album's third single, it only reached 44 in the US, but spent two weeks at number eight on the Hot Country Singles chart. Apparently, this sparked industry speculation over a possible Carpenters' country album – something Richard says the band had indeed considered in 1975, though A&M's Jerry Moss had been against the idea.

Like 'All You Get From Love is a Love Song', the US single had 'I Have You' on the B-side. The UK single was paired with 'B'wana She No Home'.

'Two Sides' (Scott E. Davis)
Continuing in a country style, this gentle ballad featured some sobbing pedal steel from Jay Dee Maness, who previously played on 'The End of the World' on *Now And Then*.

The track begins with rolling acoustic guitar from Lee Ritenour and session legend Jay Graydon: later known for his solo on Steely Dan's 'Peg' from the album *Aja*, coincidentally released on the same day as *Passage* in September 1977. The lead guitar parts are played by Tony Peluso.

The lyric is a kind of Dear John letter that reveals the breakdown of an ill-matched relationship, and also hints at two-timing. Karen harmonises with herself on the verses, and her voice is doubled on the choruses. R&B singer Lalomie Washburn gave the song a soulful interpretation on her 1978 single.

'Man Smart, Woman Smarter' (Norman Span)
This is the album's oldest composition, first recorded in 1936 by its composer the Trinidadian artist King Radio (Norman Span). Many calypso songs were written as humorous critiques on society, and the topic here is the battle of the sexes. The song has been covered many times, including versions by Harry Belafonte, Joan Baez and the cast of the TV comedy *I Love Lucy*. The Carpenters' recording most closely resembles Robert Palmer's 1976 version from his album *Some People Can Do What They Like*.

Beginning with an oddly-timed introduction, the rhythm is a jerky take on the clave rhythm typical of calypso. Creating the rich rhythms are Ed Green on drums, Tommy Vig on tambourine, and on congas, King Erisson: a legendary session musician who'd appeared on many classic Motown recordings. Joe Osborn's bass line is doubled by baritone sax, while tenor saxophonist Jackie Kelso – a veteran player for Johnny Otis, Duke Ellington and Gene Vincent – is given at least half the song to solo. Richard and Tom Hensley play tack piano, while Leon Russell makes a guest appearance, adding bluesy piano licks.

The arrangement is something of a Caribbean carnival by way of New Orleans, and Karen's vocal is bright and bubbly. Crazy sound effects add to the party atmosphere, including bird calls, train whistles, bicycle bells and wheels, all doubtlessly inspired by musical humourist Spike Jones. Richard contributes a belch to the second chorus, which also features engineer Dave Iveland's comment 'Wrong!'. Vince Charles is credited with steel drums, though these get rather lost in the overcrowded mix.

'Calling Occupants Of Interplanetary Craft (The Recognized Anthem Of World Contact Day)' (Terry Draper, John Woloschuk)
Single A-side b/w 'Can't Smile Without You'

Release date: 9 September 1977
Charts: US: 32, UK: 9

Having made trips to Nashville, the Caribbean and South America, the next ambitious destination could only be outer space. For the album's grand finale, the duo covered a progressive pop epic, originally released one year earlier by Canadian rock group Klaatu. Klaatu is the name of the alien leader who arrives on Earth by UFO in the 1951 film *The Day the Earth Stood Still*. In the story, Klaatu coincidentally chooses the name Major Carpenter when trying to blend in as a human on Earth.

The song refers to World Contact Day – an actual event from the 1950s devised by an organisation called the International Flying Saucer Bureau. At an appointed time on 15 March 1953, the bureau's followers were encouraged to telepathically send a message into space, which included the following lines:

Calling occupants of interplanetary craft that have been observing our planet EARTH. We of IFSB wish to make contact with you. We are your friends ... Please come in peace and help us in our EARTHLY problems. Give us some sign that you have received our message ...

As a science fiction fan, Richard was instantly drawn to the song. Furthermore, as a Beatles fan, he couldn't have failed to notice how much Klaatu had borrowed from The Beatles, such as the Mellotron at the beginning that recalls the intro of 'Strawberry Fields Forever'. The two bands' sound was so similar that it was even rumoured for a while that Klaatu might be The Beatles reunited and in disguise, though this theory was quickly dispelled once the band's true identities were revealed.

Klaatu's recording starts with the sound of approaching footsteps and a needle being placed on a record, while the Carpenters begin with an alien phoning a radio request show. The caller's name, Mike Ledgerwood, came from an executive at A&M's UK branch. Once again, Tony Peluso plays an overly enthusiastic DJ, while the alien voices were supplied by Richard.

Structurally, this version matches the Klaatu original, albeit shifted up a key to suit Karen's voice. In terms of the arrangement, where Klaatu's version featured just three musicians on keyboards, guitars and drums, the Carpenters' recording features around 160 musicians, including the Los Angeles Philharmonic Orchestra (led by Peter Knight) and The Gregg Smith Singers.

Subtle arrangement details include the strings mimicking a saucer as it approaches and flies away, heard behind Karen in the first chorus. Also, the flutes occurring just after the line 'We are your friends' recall the Mellotron part that opens Klaatu's version. The orchestral finale is heralded by a soaring guitar solo from Tony Peluso, starting at 4:50.

Running over seven minutes in length, the track was never intended to be a single. However, the phenomenal success of *Star Wars* in the summer of

1977 launched a space-themed craze in popular culture, and caused A&M to see new potential in the track. A four-minute edit was released in September 1977 as the album's second single, reaching 32 in the US, the top 10 in the UK and number 1 in Ireland. The single cover featured artwork by science-fiction illustrator Andrew Probert, who later created designs for the *Battlestar Galactica* TV series and *Star Trek* movies. An accompanying video was shot at Vidtronics in Hollywood, with Karen and Richard performing while they appeared to float through space. The track also became a key part of their 1978 TV special *The Carpenters...Space Encounters*.

While most compilations include the full-length album version, the single edit can be found on the collections *Carpenters – The Complete Singles* (2015) and *Japanese Single Box* (2006).

Related Tracks
'You're The One' (Steve Ferguson)
Recorded in 1977, this song was left off the *Passage* album due to its similarity to the ballad 'I Just Fall in Love Again'. It was eventually included on the *Lovelines* compilation in 1989.

Written by Steve Ferguson of the rock band NRBQ (or New Rhythm and Blues Quintet), this engaging ballad is in the style of classic standards from the Great American Songbook. Karen's voice is intimate in the verses but grows in power for the pre-chorus and chorus. The recording was one of two previously unreleased tracks (the other was 'Where Do I Go From Here?') featured in the TV movie *The Karen Carpenter Story*.

'Suntory Pop: Jingles #1 and #2' (Hiromasa Suzuki, Yoko Narahashi)
In 1977, Karen and Richard were hired to promote Pop – a new line of fruit-flavoured soft drinks from the Japanese Suntory company. The duo appeared in two TV advertisements, one showing Richard playing piano in a field while Karen throws handfuls of flower petals into the wind, and the other showing them on a yacht. Both ads had 'Top Of The World' as the soundtrack, but there were also two short radio jingles. The first starts with a breezy disco rhythm before changing to a Broadway-style show tune. The second sounds closer to the Carpenters' recognisable style, with a drum rhythm that recalls 'Only Yesterday', and a tune vaguely reminiscent of 'It's Going to Take Some Time'.

While the English lyric may sound a little stilted, the tracks are appealing, especially in their use of harmony. Karen even matches a Japanese speaker's pronunciation of the brand name Suntory. All instruments were played by Karen, Richard and Tony Peluso, and both tracks can be found on the compilations *From the Top* and *The Essential Collection: 1965-1997*.

'Leave Yesterday Behind' (Fred Karlin)
Recorded in 1978, this was composed for a made-for-TV movie of the same name. At a time when the duo were pushing in new directions, this looks

back to their past, not least with the inclusion of the word 'yesterday' in the title. Mostly, the song resembles 'For All We Know', from the opening cor anglais part to the backing vocals, and from Joe Osborn's octave-climbing bass lines to Ron Tutt's drum patterns. Unsurprisingly, both songs were composed by Fred Karlin.

The recording remained an outtake, and an entirely different arrangement was used in the TV movie, as sung by Shandi Sinnamon, who later contributed songs to the soundtracks of *Flashdance*, *The Karate Kid* and *Sailor Moon*.

Karen's vocal take on this recording is a guide vocal, and Richard completed the recording with additional orchestration and backing vocals in 1999, ahead of its 2001 release on the *As Time Goes By* compilation.

'Little Girl Blue' (Richard Rodgers, Lorenz Hart)
This song originates from the 1935 circus-themed Broadway musical *Jumbo*, and has been recorded by Frank Sinatra, Ella Fitzgerald and Nina Simone. Doris Day performed it for the 1962 film adaptation, which also starred Jimmy Durante.

The orchestra was arranged by Peter Knight, and features harpist Gayle Levant, who plays a cascading pattern in the second verse, illustrating the lyric's 'falling raindrops'. In the booklet accompanying the compilation *From the Top*, Richard states that Karen performed this jazz standard 'as if to the genre born'. This performance comes from the 1978 TV special *The Carpenters…Space Encounters,* and the track was one of two Great American Songbook pieces included on 1989's *Lovelines* compilation, along with 'When I Fall in Love'.

'Dancing In The Street' (Marvin Gaye, William 'Mickey' Stevenson, Ivy Jo Hunter)
The Richard Carpenter Trio played this song in 1968 on *Your All-American College Show*: one of their earliest TV appearances, with Karen singing, and temporary bass player Bill Sissoyev. That particular version segued into 'The Shadow of Your Smile', where Richard and Bill took solos, before returning to 'Dancing in the Street' and a closing drum solo from Karen. The performance won the competition that week, and the prizes were presented to them by Zsa Zsa Gabor, William Shatner and Frankie Avalon.

In 1978, the duo filmed another version of the song for the *The Carpenters…Space Encounters* TV special, and this recording can be found on the compilation *As Time Goes By*. This newer version was closer to the original Martha and the Vandellas hit, albeit with additional strings and a slight disco feel.

'Medley: Close Encounters/Star Wars' (John Williams)
The Carpenters…Space Encounters TV special was aired in May 1978 following the sensational popularity of the 1977 films *Star Wars* and *Close Encounters of*

the Third Kind. Coincidentally, the Carpenters had decided to record 'Calling Occupants Of Interplanetary Craft' that year, providing them with a chance hit and a legitimate excuse to choose a space theme for their third TV special.

It also made perfect sense to include the two films' soundtracks in their special, and Peter Knight was tasked with creating an arrangement that blended elements from the main and incidental themes of both films. As Richard states on the official Carpenters website, a six-minute orchestral performance would likely test the concentration powers of most viewers, so the music was accompanied by a laser-light show and various explosions: all to the detriment of the music, in Richard's opinion. The medley was released in 2001 on the compilation *As Time Goes By*.

'When I Fall In Love' (Edward Heyman, Victor Young)
This evergreen standard first emerged as an instrumental theme in the 1952 film *One Minute to Zero*. Its composer, Victor Young, also wrote 'It's Christmas Time', as included on *Christmas Portrait* (1978). Later in 1952, Edward Heyman added lyrics. Doris Day was the first to make it a hit, though it's perhaps most associated with Nat King Cole, who performed it in the 1957 film *Istanbul*.

The Carpenters' version received a lush 1950s-style orchestral treatment from Peter Knight, and the keyboards were played by Pete Jolly. It was originally recorded in 1978 for the *The Carpenters...Space Encounters* TV special, but wasn't used until 1980's *Music, Music, Music,* where it fit alongside a programme of classics from the Great American Songbook. Karen delivers a mature and considered reading of the song, once again demonstrating the ease with which she could extend her skills to a range of musical styles. The recording was first released on *Lovelines* (1989), and has subsequently appeared in remixed form on *Interpretations*, *Love Songs* and other compilations.

'Where Do I Go From Here?' (Parker McGee)
England Dan and John Ford Coley scored a number 2 hit in 1976 with the Parker McGee song 'I'd Really Love to See You Tonight'. The following year, they recorded his 'Where Do I Go From Here?' for their album *Dowdy Ferry Road*. In 1978, Barry Manilow also recorded it for his *Even Now* album, along with his version of 'Can't Smile Without You'.

In 1978, the Carpenters made several recordings that were left unreleased at the time, including this criminally overlooked song, which was finally mixed for inclusion on the 1989 compilation *Lovelines*. The song was also included in the TV biopic *The Karen Carpenter Story*.

'Honolulu City Lights' (Keola Beamer)
Single A-side b/w 'I Just Fall in Love Again'
Release date: December 1986

The writer of this sentimental mid-tempo ballad – Keola Beamer – was half of the Hawaiian Beamer duo with his brother Kapono. Richard and Karen heard the track while on vacation in Hawaii, and their arrangement begins by replicating the original's guitar and piano introduction, before taking the song in a country direction with pedal steel played by Jay Dee Maness.

The track was recorded in 1978 and remained an outtake, with orchestral parts added in April 1983 – suggesting Richard possibly considered it for the *Voice Of The Heart* album. It was released as a single in 1986 but didn't chart. It was subsequently included on 1989's *Lovelines* compilation.

'Slow Dance' (Philip Margo, Mitchell Margo)

This smooth, easygoing number was written by brothers Margo who in 1961 had scored a hit with 'The Lion Sleeps Tonight' as members of the doo-wop group The Tokens (an earlier lineup of which had included Neil Sedaka), Richard and Karen's Christmas TV special guests Kristy and Jimmy McNichol released a version of 'Slow Dance' in 1978. The Carpenters began recording their own version in 1978, laying down rhythm tracks. The track was then shelved until 1980 when woodwinds were added, which presumably included the flute solo by John Phillips. Given the timing of the sessions, the song was no doubt considered for 1981's *Made In America,* where the song title coincidentally appears in the opening lines of 'Touch Me When We're Dancing'. Strings and horns were added in early 1983, suggesting that the track was also considered for that year's *Voice Of The Heart* album, though it eventually saw release on 1989's *Lovelines.*

Christmas Portrait (1978)

Personnel:
Karen Carpenter: vocals
Richard Carpenter: vocals, keyboards
Pete Jolly: keyboards
Joe Osborn: bass
Ron Tutt, Cubby O'Brien: drums
Bob Bain, Tony Peluso, Tommy Tedesco: guitars
Gayle Levant, Dorothy Remsen: harp
Earle Dumler, John Ellis: oboe
Bob Messenger: Tenor saxophone
The Tom Bahler Chorale: vocals
Engineered by Ray Gerhardt, Roger Young and Dave Iveland
'Merry Christmas Darling' produced by Jack Daugherty
Special Thanks to Ed Sulzer
Produced by Richard Carpenter
Associate Producer: Karen Carpenter
Orchestral Arrangements by Peter Knight, Billy May and Richard Carpenter
Recorded at A&M Studios, Hollywood, CA
Release date: 13 October 1978
Label: A&M
Charts: US: 145 (56 in 2020) UK: 104
Running Time 49:08

Though the last two albums had only been moderately successful, *The Carpenters' Very First TV Special* scored top-10 ratings in December 1976, and the ABC network asked them to follow it with a Christmas special in 1977. Production for *Carpenters at Christmas* began in August that year, co-starring comedy actor Harvey Korman, teenage actress Kristy McNichol and Burr Tillstrom's puppets Kukla and Ollie. As they worked on the show, it became obvious there should be an accompanying album, to follow in the tradition of festive albums by Perry Como, Bing Crosby, Nat King Cole, Phil Spector, The Beach Boys and others. This took longer than anticipated, and it would be October 1978 before *Christmas Portrait* was finally released. The lengthy sessions resulted in nearly enough material for two albums (leftovers forming a significant portion of the 1984 album *An Old-Fashioned Christmas*), and for the duo's second Christmas TV special, *The Carpenters: A Christmas Portrait*, broadcast in 1978. This show featured Gene Kelly, comedy actress Georgia Engel from *The Mary Tyler Moore Show*, illusionist Peter Pit, and Kristy McNichol again, this time appearing with her brother Jimmy. The recording sessions had to be scheduled around other commitments, such as the 1977 Christmas residency at the MGM Grand in Las Vegas. For these concerts, they brought in a giant Christmas tree and filled the stage with almost 80 musicians, including a 24-piece choir, as they tested out some of their new seasonal repertoire.

Returning to A&M's Studio D, most of the recording took place outside the festive period, though Karen still found it easy to summon the Christmas spirit due to her close affinity for the season. In fact, she and Richard had been planning a Christmas album since they first signed with A&M in 1969, but so far had only released two Christmas singles: 'Merry Christmas, Darling' and 'Santa Claus is Comin' to Town'. Richard added the following dedication to 1984's *An Old-Fashioned Christmas:*

This album is lovingly dedicated to the memory of my late sister and friend Karen, who was extremely fond of both Christmas and Christmas music.

Both Carpenters' Christmas albums are clearly influenced by Spike Jones' 1956 *Xmas Spectacular* album: a childhood favourite for the duo. Though Jones was best known for novelty songs, *Xmas Spectacular* included both straight and comic Christmas songs, performed by his City Slickers band and The Jud Conlon Singers. Richard was such a fan of Jud Conlon's vocal arrangements that he attempted to hire him for Carpenter's sessions before he discovered that Conlon had died in 1966.

Great care was taken over the material for both albums, mixing religious and secular Christmas favourites, and sequencing each song to flow neatly into the next. There's a nostalgia to both collections, captured by the Norman Rockwell-style cover art, which on *Christmas Portrait* references Rockwell's 1960 painting 'Triple Self-Portrait'. Presumably, Rockwell was unavailable to do the cover himself, having stopped painting in 1976 at the age of 82. He passed away in November 1978: a month after the album's release. The pastiche cover was instead designed by movie poster artist Robert Tanenbaum, whose surname coincidentally translates from German as Christmas tree.

Richard took a production role on this album, but was less involved in arranging, playing and singing due to the problems he was facing with his Quaalude addiction. As a result, the trademark Carpenters sound was replaced with the orchestration of Peter Knight, and the jazz arrangements of Billy May. Richard's involvement was so reduced that he considers *Christmas Portrait* to be a Karen Carpenter solo record.

Though well-received by critics, the album reached 145 in the US charts but remained a seasonal favourite with fans, going platinum by 1998. The album re-charted in the US in 2020, reaching number 56. The 1984 CD release was a special edition increasing the running time from 49 minutes to 74, interspersing selections from *An Old-Fashioned Christmas*. Richard later remixed four songs for the 1990 compilation *From The Top*, creating further remixes in 1992 for the two-CD Time Life compilation *Christmas with The Carpenters*. This included a subtly different version of 'Merry Christmas, Darling' with re-recorded stereo piano and new reverb on Karen's voice.

Christmas Portrait and *An Old-Fashioned Christmas* were finally issued on CD in their full original running orders in 1996 as the double-package *Christmas Collection*, using the reverb-heavy 1992 remixes for almost all of the *Christmas Portrait* material, but the original 1984 mixes for *An Old-Fashioned Christmas*.

'O Come, O Come Emmanuel' (Trad. Arr. Richard Carpenter)

The album opens with an 8th-century advent hymn traditionally sung by monks in the week leading up to Christmas. Each day had its own hymn and used a different name for Jesus, the name Emmanuel meaning 'God with us' in Hebrew. The words were translated from Latin in 1851 by English priest John Mason Neale, who was also the author of 'Good King Wenceslas' (included on *An Old-Fashioned Christmas*). Around the time of Neale's translation, the lyrics were combined with the familiar melody (derived from a 15th-century French requiem mass).

Richard's brief *a cappella* performance is a prelude to the album overture that flows on from his final note. In the 1992 remix, the words 'and ransom' became 'shall ransom', taken from an alternative vocal take.

'Overture'
A. **'Deck The Halls (With Boughs Of Holly)'** (Trad. French carol)
B. **'I Saw Three Ships'** (Trad. Welsh carol, Arr. David Overton)
C. **'Have Yourself A Merry Little Christmas'** (Hugh Martin, Ralph Blane)
D. **'God Rest Ye Merry Gentlemen'** (Trad. English carol)
E. **'Away In A Manger (Luther's Cradle Hymn)'** (Anon., James Ramsey Murray)
F. **'What Child Is This?' ('Greensleeves')** (English air, William Chatterton Dix)
G. **'Carol Of The Bells'** (Trad. Ukrainian carol, Arr. Nick Perito, Peter Knight)
H. **'O Come All Ye Faithful'** (Adeste Fideles) (English version: Frederick Oakeley, John Francis Wade, John Reading)

The instrumental overture consists of Peter Knight's lively orchestral arrangements of eight familiar Christmas songs. Starting with a sprightly version of 'Deck the Halls' – a 16th-century melody to which words were added in the 19th century – moving quickly to 'I Saw Three Ships': a 17th-century tune, again with a 19th-century lyric. Next comes 'Have Yourself a Merry Little Christmas' (which contains a brief quote from 'Jingle Bells'). This is the newest of the overture selections and the medley's only non-carol, having been introduced in the 1994 film *Meet Me in St. Louis*, where it was sung by Judy Garland. Karen sings it in full later in the album.

The pace then steps up for the 17th-century carol 'God Rest Ye Merry Gentlemen'. This sprightly arrangement briefly becomes a brassy Vegas-style show tune before the tempo slows for 'Away in a Manger': an American carol from the 19th century. Various melodies have been composed for this carol, though this one is known as the 'Mueller' tune, and is probably the most familiar to American listeners. The overture moves next to 'What Child is This?'

– a carol combining a 19th-century lyric with the 16th-century English folk tune of 'Greensleeves'.

This is followed by 'Carol of the Bells' – a Ukrainian folk tune traditionally sung on New Year's Eve – before finishing with a verse of 'O Come All Ye Faithful'. The origin of this carol is uncertain, though it's thought to be from the 18th century. The arrangement develops from a quiet and stately verse into a grandiose finale, where the tempo slows and it modulates to the key of the next track.

'The Christmas Waltz' (Sammy Cahn, Jule Styne)

Karen's voice now appears for the first time on this 1950s Christmas classic. The duo also opened their 1978 TV special *The Carpenters: A Christmas Portrait* with the song. The songwriters Cahn and Styne also wrote the evergreen 'Let it Snow! Let it Snow! Let it Snow!', heard later on the album. 'The Christmas Waltz' was originally written for Frank Sinatra, and has since been covered by Andy Williams, Harry Connick Jr., Norah Jones and others.

'Sleigh Ride' (Mitchell Parish, Leroy Anderson)

Songwriter Leroy Anderson first performed this high-spirited tune in the 1940s as an instrumental. He also wrote 'The Typewriter' – a zany piece for orchestra and typewriter featured in the 1963 Jerry Lewis film *Who's Minding the Store?*. The lyric was added in 1950 by Mitchell Parish, who also wrote the lyrics for the standards 'Stardust', 'Deep Purple' and 'Moonlight Serenade'. Like 'The Christmas Waltz', 'Sleigh Ride' has a nostalgic feel, describing an idyllic Christmas in a small rural community as if from a picture by Currier and Ives: the 19th-century printing firm who specialised in Americana scenes. 'Sleigh Ride' was previously recorded by The Andrews Sisters, Bing Crosby and Ella Fitzgerald, and by The Ronettes on the 1963 Phil Spector album *A Christmas Gift For You*.

The Carpenters' version begins with Karen's unaccompanied voice. The 1992 remix uses an alternate vocal take for this section. Brushes set the upbeat tempo with a rhythm that mimics the trotting of horses. Additional vocals come from the Tom Bahler chorus, and Bob Messenger, Doug Strawn and Richard, who arrive in turn to announce a party at the home of one Farmer Grey. The middle section ends with a challenging melody sequence that Karen was anxious to get right. As encouragement, arranger Billy May wrote the words 'Take it, Baby' over this line on her vocal score, and she then sang it flawlessly on the first take, according to Richard in Lennox and May's book on the group.

'Sleigh Ride' was chosen as the opening number for the 1977 *Carpenters at Christmas* TV special.

'It's Christmas Time'/'Sleep Well, Little Children' (Victor Young, Al Stillman)/(Alan Bergman, Leon Klatzkin)

This medley comes from the 1956 Spike Jones album *A Christmas Spectacular*, and pairs an upbeat number with a charming ballad. Composer

Victor Young wrote the standards 'Love Letters', 'My Foolish Heart' and '(I Don't Stand) A Ghost of a Chance with You'. Lyricist Al Stillman wrote 'I Believe', and the Christmas song '(There's No Place Like) Home for the Holidays' included on *An Old-Fashioned Christmas*.

Maintaining the prior song's tempo, 'It's Christmas Time' begins with Karen accompanied by lively baroque-style piano. This opening segment was included in *The Carpenters at Christmas* TV special. Peter Knight adds a light orchestral accompaniment beneath the choir part borrowed from the Spike Jones original, along with tinkling sleigh bells and triangle.

The tempo then slows for 'Sleep Well, Little Children': a lullaby waltz to calm excited children on the night before Christmas. The music was written by 1950s TV composer Leon Klatzkin (known for *Gunsmoke* and *Rawhide*), and lyricist Alan Bergman had co-written 'The Way We Were', 'The Windmills of Your Mind' and 'What Are You Doing the Rest of Your Life?'.

The Carpenters were guests on the 1974 TV special *Perry Como's Christmas Show,* which included both these Christmas numbers, with Karen and Como singing 'Sleep Well, Little Children' as a duet.

'Have Yourself A Merry Little Christmas' (Hugh Martin, Ralph Blane)

This well-loved Christmas song comes from the 1944 Judy Garland musical *Meet Me in St. Louis*, (for which the songwriters Martin and Blane also created 'The Trolley Song'). Written during the turmoil of World War II, the original version reflected the era in lines like 'It may be your last'. For his 1957 album *A Jolly Christmas*, Frank Sinatra requested the line 'Until then we'll have to muddle through somehow' be rewritten, and it became 'Hang a shining star upon the highest bough'.

Billy May arranged an appropriately languid backing for Karen's warmhearted vocal.

'Santa Claus Is Comin' To Town' (Haven Giliespie, John Frederick Coots)

The tempo picks up again as the choir and Karen sing a brief excerpt from this 1930s Christmas classic. This version was included in the 1978 TV special *The Carpenters: A Christmas Portrait*, while the 1974 single version is used on their second Christmas album, *An Old-Fashioned Christmas*.

'The Christmas Song (Chestnuts Roasting On An Open Fire)' (Mel Tormé, Robert Wells)

A-side b/w 'Merry Christmas, Darling'
Single Release date: 11 November 1978
Jazz singer Mel Tormé and composer Robert Wells worked on this song in summer 1945, and a straightforward version appeared on Spike Jones' *Xmas Spectacular* album. The light-jazz arrangement here was by Billy May, and

Karen's enjoyment of the song and the subject it celebrates comes across clearly in her vocals.

It was released as a single shortly after the album came out, though it didn't chart. The B-side 'Merry Christmas, Darling' featured a new lead vocal from Karen, who was never happy with her original vocal.

For the 1977 TV special *Carpenters at Christmas*, Karen performs 'The Christmas Song' sitting wrapping gifts by the fireside.

'Silent Night' (Franz Gruber, Arr. Peter Knight)

Side one finishes with one of the best-known Christmas carols, written in 1818 by Austrian composer Franz Gruber, who adapted the poem 'Stille Nacht' by Catholic priest Father Joseph Mohr.

Peter Knight created a gentle and atmospheric backing with choir, strings, tubular bells and delicate harp, Karen ending on a low E. On the 1978 TV special *The Carpenters: A Christmas Portrait*, she sang the song in German with guest star Georgia Engel.

'Jingle Bells' (James Pierpont, Arr. Peter Knight)

Side two begins with a sprightly and lighthearted version of this Christmas classic, which dates to the 1850s and was written by James Lord Piermont (uncle of investment banker J. P. Morgan), who was inspired by the sleigh races of his native Massachusetts.

In the 1978 TV special *The Carpenters: A Christmas Portrait*, 'Jingle Bells' is paired with 'Santa Claus is Comin' to Town' in a comedy scene where Karen prepares party food at home.

'The First Snowfall'/'Let It Snow' (Medley) (Paul Francis Webster, Joseph F. Burke)/(Sammy Cahn, Jule Styne)

This jolly medley was adapted from the Spike Jones *Xmas Spectacular* album. 'The First Snowfall' includes a brief quote from 'Jingle Bells' in the final verse.

The composer for 'The First Snowfall' was bandleader Sonny Burke, who co-wrote the song for the film *Lady and the Tramp* with Peggy Lee. Lyricist Paul Francis Webster wrote 'The Shadow of Your Smile', 'Love is a Many Splendored Thing' and Doris Day's hit 'Secret Love'. Cahn and Styne also wrote 'The Christmas Waltz' on this album.

'Carol Of The Bells' (Trad. Ukrainian carol, Arr. Richard Carpenter)

Richard takes to the piano on this spellbinding carol based on the Ukrainian folk song 'Shchedryk', which celebrated the coming of the Ukrainian New Year, which was in spring rather than December. The lyric tells of a swallow arriving at a house to predict a bountiful year ahead. The tune was given a new interpretation in the 1930s by Peter Wilhousky – an American composer of Ukrainian descent – who thought the melody evoked the sound of handbells.

Richard had performed the song with a small choir on *Perry Como's Christmas Show* in 1974.

'Merry Christmas Darling' (Frank Pooler, Richard Carpenter)

The album's only Carpenter composition was originally a single in 1970, details of which can be found in the Related Tracks section of the *Close To You* chapter. Unhappy with the timbre of her original vocal, Karen re-recorded it for this album in 1978. The original single can be heard on the compilations *From the Top* and *The Essential Collection: 1965-1997*.

For their 1978 TV special *The Carpenters: A Christmas Portrait,* Karen sings the song walking across snow to post a Christmas card.

'I'll Be Home For Christmas' (Kim Gannon, Walter Kent, Buck Ram)

Continuing the theme of letters sent to loved ones at Christmas, this lyric is from the perspective of a soldier stationed far from home. Bing Crosby's 1943 wartime recording was popular with servicemen and civilians alike, achieving gold status. Many artists have recorded the song, including Frank Sinatra, Elvis Presley, The Beach Boys and The Osmonds.

Lyricist Kim Gannon was an attorney who also wrote the charming 'Moonlight Cocktail' for Glenn Miller, while Walter Kent had written '(There'll be Bluebirds Over) the White Cliffs of Dover', among others. Buck Ram – manager of The Platters – was credited because of a court case over a similarly-titled composition.

'Christ Is Born' (Ray Charles, Domenico Bartolucci)

Richard first heard this enchanting song on *The Perry Como Christmas Album* (1968). The original Italian lyric was by Monsignor Bartolucci: a director of the Sistine Chapel Choir. The English lyric was by Ray Charles: the conductor of Como's backing-vocal group.

The expanded choral sound came from combining the Tom Bahler Chorale with the Carpenters' former choir from CSULB.

The song appears in *The Carpenters at Christmas* 1977 TV special, and the studio recording was remixed in 1990 for inclusion on *From the Top* and *The Essential Collection: 1965-1997*.

'Medley'
 A. **'Winter Wonderland'** (Richard B. Smith, Felix Bernard)
 B. **'Silver Bells'** (Jay Livingston, Ray Evans)
 C. **'White Christmas'** (Irving Berlin)

'Winter Wonderland' was written in 1934 by pianist Felix Bernard, who also wrote for Al Jolson, Eddie Cantor and Sophie Tucker. The lyric was by Smith who tragically died of tuberculosis the following year at the age of 34.

This is another medley from Spike Jones' *Xmas Spectacular*, that version being the basis for Billy May's arrangement, beginning with bright trumpets leading into an upbeat show tune-style arrangement. In Jones' version, the snowman is imagined as a circus clown, but Karen sings the original lyric where the snowman is a chaplain.

The tempo then slows to a waltz for 'Silver Bells', written in 1950 by the team behind the classics 'To Each His Own', 'Mona Lisa' and 'Que Sera Sera (Whatever Will Be, Will Be)'. While Spike Jones recorded a straightforward rendition, this is a comic interpretation with madcap xylophone, clanging tubular bells and a sagging trombone – as per *The Carpenters at Christmas* 1977 TV special.

The medley ends with Irving Berlin's 'White Christmas', which appeared in the Bing Crosby films *Holiday Inn* (1942) and *White Christmas* (1954). The nostalgic lyric was an instant success with homesick World War II soldiers. The TV special version begins with the line 'I'm dreaming of a White Christmas', while this recording starts with the original introductory verse.

The medley ends with a short solo piano segue into the closing number 'Ave Maria'. This part was originally played on the same Fender Rhodes piano as 'Ave Maria', but Richard re-recorded it on a Yamaha DX7 synthesizer in 1992 for the Time Life compilation *Christmas with The Carpenters*, changing again to acoustic piano for the 1996 *Christmas Collection* set.

'Ave Maria' (Johann Sebastian Bach, Adapted by Charles Gounod, Arr. Peter Knight)
This Christian prayer has been set to music by some of the most famous composers in classical music, including Schubert, Mozart, Liszt, Brahms and Stravinsky. The version here by 19th-century French composer Gounod pairs a new melody with 'Prelude No.1': the opening piece from Bach's 18th-century collection *The Well-Tempered Clavier*.

Karen sings a Latin lyric based on the Gospel of Luke, which essentially translates as follows:

Hail Mary, full of grace, the Lord is with thee
Blessed art thou amongst women
And blessed is the fruit of thy womb, Jesus
Holy Mary, pray for us sinners
Now and at the hour of our death
Amen

The recitation of the Hail Mary prayer is commonly accompanied by the ringing of bells, and tubular bells are heard here after the words 'Sancta Maria'.

Karen's interpretation is captivating throughout. In the studio, she was joined by The Tom Bahler Chorale, though these tapes went missing, so the original *Christmas Portrait* had Karen by herself. A 48-piece choir was overdubbed in 1984, and that mix has been used on all subsequent editions. With the album being bookended with religious pieces (each sung by a different sibling), this magical rendition of 'Ave Maria' completes this comprehensive festive collection, just as it concluded their 1978 TV special *The Carpenters: Christmas Portrait*. The track was remixed in 1990 for *From the Top* and *The Essential Collection: 1965-1997*.

Related Tracks
'Lovelines' (Rod Temperton)
'Lovelines' provided the title for the Carpenters' second compilation of unreleased material, released in 1989. The song also became the opening track on Karen's posthumous 1996 solo album, recorded in New York with producer Phil Ramone. More information on the *Karen Carpenter* album can be found in the Solo Albums and Reinterpretations chapter.

The track's disco rhythm is one of the new musical styles that Karen explored under the guidance of producer Phil Ramone when recording her solo album in 1979. The prominent bass part was played by Louis Johnson of The Brothers Johnson, while the dexterous Fender Rhodes solo comes from Greg Phillinganes – both of whom played on Michael Jackson's *Off the Wall* album the same year. Songwriter Rod Temperton contributed three songs to Jackson's album, and adds innovative vocal and rhythmic parts to this track. The flutes and strings were orchestrated by jazz pianist Bob James, composer of 'Angela': the theme tune for the comedy TV series *Taxi*.

When Karen first told Richard of her plans for a solo album, he warned her to avoid disco, as he saw it as a passing fad and one that didn't suit her image or vocal style. Given his position, it may seem odd that ten years later, he remixed this and other disco tracks by Karen for the Carpenters' *Lovelines* compilation. However, Richard has also said these were the tracks from her solo album that Karen was most pleased with, and presumably, he wanted to fulfil her wish to see them released.

'If We Try' (Rod Temperton)
Another track recorded for Karen's solo album, and first issued on the *Lovelines* compilation. This sophisticated, breezy disco ballad features smooth vocals and an intricate brass arrangement from Rod Temperton. The track could easily belong to the 1970s R&B subgenre known as Quiet Storm – a radio format of laid-back tracks like Bobby Caldwell's 'What You Won't Do For Love', and Heatwave's 'Always and Forever' (also written by Rod Temperton).

'If I Had You' (Stephen Dorff, Gary Harju, Larry Herbstritt)
Single A-side b/w 'The Uninvited Guest'
Release date: November 1989
This striking disco number was the third of four songs from Karen's solo album to be selected for the 1989 *Lovelines* compilation. 'If I Had You' was written by the duo's friend Stephen Dorff, who, with Larry Herbstritt, had

written 'I Just Fall in Love Again' on *Passage*. Joining with Gary Harju, the trio had also written songs for Cher and Melissa Manchester.

Richard has named this song as his personal favourite from Karen's solo recordings. Rod Temperton is credited with 'vocal acrobatics', and Richard recalls Karen phoning him from New York exclaiming how challenging the backing vocals had been. The orchestral arrangement – which switches from long sustained chords in the verses to short staccato string-and-brass stabs in the chorus – was by in-demand trumpeter Jerry Hey, who also played on Michael Jackson's *Off the Wall*. The seductive saxophone intro and solo were played by Michael Brecker, and the core group of guitarist Russell Javors, bassist Doug Stegmeyer and drummer Liberty DeVitto came from Billy Joel's band. When Richard remixed the track in 1989, he had Joe Osborn replace Stegmeyer's bass part, and replaced the original fade-out with an innovative ending taken from Karen's syncopated backing vocals.

'Remember When Lovin' Took All Night' (John Farrar, Molly-Ann Leiken)

This slick disco track intended for Karen's solo LP was written by John Farrar, who supplied four number-one hits for Karen's friend Olivia Newton-John, including 'Hopelessly Devoted to You' and 'You're the One That I Want' from the 1978 movie musical *Grease*. His co-writer Molly-Ann Leiken had written for Anne Murray, Billie Jo Spears and Yvonne Elliman, and written with songwriters Albert Hammond and Stephen Dorff.

The arrangement is filled with unexpected, thrilling moments, from the intro's sudden chromatic dip in the backing vocals to the abrupt shift to a new key in the pre-chorus, and the Latin breakdown in the outro. Perhaps the most unexpected thing is hearing Karen singing lyrics like 'I feel your eyes starting a fire all over me' and groaning on the fade-out. While such things now seem tame, they were very much at odds with Karen's image at the time.

Nevertheless, Karen's vocals have spirit, and match the energy of Airto Moreira's percussion and arranger Bob James' Rhodes piano solo. Richard remixed the track in 1989.

'My Body Keeps Changing My Mind' (Leslie Pearl)

This disco number from Karen's solo album includes almost every characteristic of the genre, with punchy brass, perky flutes, mandatory handclaps and all the rest. Around the time she recorded this track, Johnny Mathis released a slightly faster version on his 1979 album *Mathis Magic*.

Songwriter Leslie Pearl later worked with Crystal Gayle, Mary MacGregor, and Karen Kamon aka Karen Ichiuji-Ramone, who was Phil Ramone's wife and Karen's friend.

Possibly the most danceable song in the Carpenters' catalogue, this track, in particular, seems to bear out Richard's prediction that disco would soon sound out-of-date. No doubt this factor and the sensual lyric explain why it wasn't selected for *Lovelines*. However, this track and 'Still Crazy After All These Years' (also cut for the solo album) provided exclusive content for the 1991 rarities compilation *From the Top*.

'Still Crazy After All These Years' (Paul Simon)

Phil Ramone produced this song for its composer Paul Simon in 1975, and recommended it to Karen. Keyboardist Rob Mounsey made a new, slightly slower arrangement, stretching Simon's waltz rhythm into a 6/8 blues. It's arguable whether Karen suited a song like this, as her good-natured reading seems to bypass the existential unease of Simon's original. Indeed, Karen was uncomfortable singing the words 'crapped out', changing them to 'crashed out'.

'I Got Rhythm Medley' (George Gershwin, Ira Gershwin)

Released on the 2001 compilation *As Time Goes By*, this medley was originally devised for the 1980 TV special *Music, Music, Music*. It featured a soft-shoe routine from Karen and four male dancers, plus her drum solo over Gershwin's 'Fascinating Rhythm', 'S'Wonderful' and 'Rhapsody in Blue'. The closing belch comes from Richard.

'Without A Song' (Edward Eliscu, Billy Rose, Vincent Youmans)

This entrancing piece came from the 1929 Broadway musical *Great Day*, which also featured the enduring standard 'More Than You Know'. Subsequent versions were recorded by Duke Ellington, Tony Bennett, Frank Sinatra and others.

The Carpenters' version opened the *Music, Music, Music*. TV special. It starts with the duo's multitracked *a cappella* choir in a style similar to The Beach Boys. Guests Ella Fitzgerald and John Davidson sing the central section, before all four singers join for the final verse and the grand ending with orchestra and choir.

Following the filming of the special, Richard and Karen remixed the show's mono recordings in stereo for their own personal collections, replacing their guests' vocals with their own, and creating a full uninterrupted version, which was released on the 2001 compilation *As Time Goes By*. An edit of the *a cappella* introduction was used as the opening track of the 1994 compilation *Interpretations*.

'Dizzy Fingers' (Zez Confrey)

'Dizzy Fingers' is a frantic novelty piano song written in 1923 following writer Zez Confrey's earlier success with 'Kitten on the Keys'. Pianists like Liberace and Winnifred Atwell have employed it as an ostentatious showstopper, while Benny Goodman adapted it for the clarinet, and Chet Atkins for the guitar.

Richard had performed the song solo for several years before including it in the TV special *Music, Music, Music*. There, he was joined by an orchestra, using the same arrangement created for the 1956 film *The Eddy Duchin Story*. As if the song wasn't already zany enough, Richard ups the ante by playing each section on a different keyboard – dashing from a grand piano to an upright, a Yamaha CP80 electric grand, a harpsichord, a toy piano and finally to another grand piano. This performance was released on the 2001 compilation *As Time Goes By*.

'You're Just In Love' (Irving Berlin)

This lighthearted duet comes from the 1950 musical *Call Me Madam* and was first performed by Broadway legends Ethel Merman and Russell Nype. It was also a hit for Perry Como with The Fontane Sisters, and Guy Mitchell with Rosemary Clooney.

The song was given a country makeover for the *Music, Music, Music* TV special and features practically the same pedal steel intro part that was played on the *Made In America* opening track 'Those Good Old Dreams', except here the key is a tone higher. Originally sung as a duet by John Davidson and Karen, Richard replaced Davidson's vocal himself for the *As Time Goes By* version.

'Karen/Ella Medley' (Leon Russell, Richard Rodgers/Lorenz Hart, Sammy Fain/Irving Kahal, George Gershwin/Ira Gershwin, Herman Hupfeld, Duke Ellington/Bob Russell, Duke Ellington/Irving Mills)

Another excerpt from the 1980 *Music, Music, Music* TV special, and also included on the *As Time Goes By* compilation, this medley consists of seven jazz standards sung by Karen with Ella Fitzgerald. It begins with Leon Russell's 'This Masquerade', before Karen sings Rodgers & Hart's 'My Funny Valentine' from the 1937 musical *Babes in Arms*. Fitzgerald had issued several live recordings of this song, and also a studio recording on her 1956 album *Ella Fitzgerald Sings the Rodgers & Hart Songbook*.

Ella then takes over on 'I'll Be Seeing You' from the flop 1938 musical *Right This Way* – though it was later made popular by Frank Sinatra, Bing Crosby and Billie Holiday. Karen follows with the Gershwins' 'Someone to Watch Over Me' – first performed by Gertrude Lawrence in the 1926 musical *Oh, Kay!*, and recorded by Fitzgerald for her 1950 album *Ella Sings Gershwin*.

We then reach Herman Hupfeld's 'As Time Goes By'. Written in 1931, it was best known from the 1942 Humphrey Bogart and Ingrid Bergman film *Casablanca*, and Karen and Ella sing it here as a duet.

The medley concludes with two simultaneous Duke Ellington numbers – 'Don't Get Around Much Anymore' and 'I Let a Song Go Out of My Heart' – both of which were recorded by Fitzgerald and Ellington on her 1957 album, *Ella Fitzgerald Sings the Duke Ellington Song Book*.

'From This Moment On' (Cole Porter)
This was an outtake from *The Carpenters: Music, Music, Music* TV Special.
Like the performance on the 1976 album *Live at the Palladium*, it features
Richard's piano and Karen's voice, combining Bach's 'Prelude No 2 in C
Minor' with Cole Porter's tune. Porter's song was featured in the musical *Kiss
Me Kate*, and had been recorded by Doris Day, Anita O'Day, Ella Fitzgerald
and others.

This recording was included on the 1994 compilation *Interpretations*.

'1980 Medley' (Joe Raposo, Burt Bacharach/Hal David, Richard
Carpenter/John Bettis, Paul Williams/Roger Nichols)
Music, Music, Music concluded with this medley of the classic Carpenters
songs 'Sing', 'Knowing When to Leave', 'Make It Easy on Yourself',
'Someday' and 'We've Only Just Begun'. Karen was especially pleased to
have the opportunity to re-record her vocal for 'Someday', always having
been unhappy with her performance on *Offering/Ticket To Ride*. The TV
performance was released as the '1980 Medley' on *From the Top* and *The
Essential Collection: 1965-1997*.

Made In America (1981)

Personnel:
Karen Carpenter: lead and backing vocals, drums and percussion (8), percussion (1)
Richard Carpenter: orchestration, backing vocals, piano, Fender Rhodes,
Wurlitzer electric piano, celesta, ARP Odyssey, arranger (5, 10)
Tim May, Tony Peluso, Fred Tackett, Dennis Budimir: guitars
Jay Dee Maness: pedal steel
Earle Dumler: oboe
Tom Scott: tenor saxophone
Gayle Levant: concert harp
Joe Osborn: bass
Larrie Londin, Ron Tutt, John Robinson: drums
Paulinho da Costa, Peter Limonick, Bob Conti: percussion
Jerry Steinholtz: congas (6)
Carolyn Dennis, Stephanie Spruill, Maxine Willard Waters: background vocals
The O.K. Chorale: backing vocals (10)
Ron Hicklin: choir director
Frank Pooler: choir conductor (10)
Peter Knight: orchestration (10)
Paul Riser: arranger and orchestration (6)
Daryl Dragon, Ian Underwood: synthesizer programming (3)
Jimmy Getzoff, Jerry Vinci: concertmaster
Produced by Richard Carpenter
Recorded at A&M
Engineered by Roger Young, Dave Iveland
'I Believe You' engineered by Ray Gerhardt
Mix engineers: Roger Young, Stewart Whitmore
Special thanks to Gary Sims, Pat Peters, Ron Gorow, John Bettis, Jules Chaikin,
Herb, Jerry, Gil and the entire A&M family.
Release date: 16 June 1981
Label: A&M
Charts: US: 52 UK: 12
Running Time 40:22

On 3 December 1978, the duo took part in the Winter Festival Concert at California State University, Long Beach, performing songs from *Christmas Portrait* with their former teacher Frank Pooler and the choir. This was to be their very last live appearance in the United States.

When *Made In America* and its lead single 'Touch Me When We're Dancing' appeared in June 1981, fans had been waiting almost three years for new material. *Made In America* was the last Carpenters album released in Karen's lifetime.

Since their last album in 1978, Richard had spent a year recovering from his Quaalude addiction, while Karen went to New York to record a solo album (discussed in the Solo Albums chapter of this book). The final mixes for Karen's record were complete by mid-March 1980, but A&M turned it down. It did not see a release until 1996.

In early 1980, Richard felt ready to return to work, and one of their first commitments was to film the TV special *Music, Music, Music*, which aired in May 1980. Sessions for *Made In America* started later that year, and ran to the following February. Recording was paused while Karen took time off to get married and have a honeymoon. Karen had met real estate developer Tom Burris in April 1980, getting engaged in June and marrying in August. Sadly, the marriage was an unhappy one, and the couple split in November 1981. Karen filed for divorce in October 1982.

Made In America was less experimental than 1977's *Passage*, returning to a familiar mixture of pop, ballads, country and golden oldies. But there was a noticeable attempt to update their sound with synthesizers, backing singers and influences from contemporary R&B. They also moved to recording on 48-track, though there were errors in synchronising the two 24-track tape machines, causing costly delays.

On its release, *Made In America* climbed to only 52 in the US. It failed to reach even silver status and was their lowest charting album since the 1969 debut. It fared slightly better overseas. It reached 12 in the UK, though none of its four singles were hits there.

The album cover was painted by airbrush illustrator David Willardson, who'd also created sleeves for Liberace, Rainbow, and The Beach Boys' *Carl and the Passions* album. The sleeve shows happy, healthy-looking portraits of Karen and Richard, stylised as artwork painted on World War II bombers. Indeed, Karen's hair appears to fly in the wind, flowing over onto the back sleeve. As it happens, this was not Willardson's first Carpenters' cover commission, as he had previously been hired in 1970 to illustrate the album *Close To You*. Since he knew nothing about them, he followed the brief given by the A&M art director, who dismissively referred to the duo as 'very vanilla'. Willardson interpreted this literally, illustrating an ice cream cone dropped onto the group photo. Unsurprisingly, this illustration was rejected.

'Those Good Old Dreams' (Richard Carpenter, John Bettis)
Single A-side b/w 'When It's Gone (It's Just Gone)'
Release date: 5 November 1981
Charts: US: 63
The album opens with a new Carpenter/Bettis collaboration, their first on record since 1976. While the sound may be cleaner and crisper than earlier releases, this song is all about looking back to cherished memories, as if to reassure listeners that the old-style pre-*Passage* Carpenters are back.

The country rhythm and instrumentation are instantly familiar, with Karen's vocals sounding as warm and reassuring as ever. Jay Dee Maness returns to play pedal steel, while Richard adds a rolling electric piano pattern that's taken up by an uncredited banjo player on the chorus. Karen can be heard on percussion along with Brazilian percussionist Paulinho Da Costa, whose credits included Dizzy Gillespie, Earth, Wind & Fire and Michael Jackson.

The track became the fourth of the album's five singles, reaching 63 on *Billboard*. A video was made, showing the album being manufactured at the pressing plant, then moving to the band playing on a colourful set hung with empty picture frames. At the chorus, the empty frames fill with black-and-white photos of Karen and Richard as children. The video used the track's original mix, which included a high-pitched pedal steel swoop part just after the final chorus. For the 1985 remix, this part is absent, as heard on the 1985 compilation *Yesterday Once More* and all subsequent releases.

'Strength Of A Woman' (Phyllis Brown, Juanita Curiel)
Eloise Laws hit 33 on the R&B chart in 1980 with a version of this song that featured an insistent string riff and light disco percussion. Songwriter Phyllis Brown had written for soul artist Ann Peebles, and her co-writer Juanita Curiel was a member of the female trio Hot, who scored a 1977 hit with 'Angel in Your Arms'.

'Strength of a Woman' opens with the familiar sound of Earle Dumler on oboe, though the soul ingredients are new to the Carpenters' sound, and may have been inspired by Karen's solo recordings. The two drummers are Ron Tutt, who'd played with the band since *Passage* in 1977, and Larrie Londin, who had experience drumming for Motown and Nashville acts. Karen is joined by three female backing singers, amusingly named The Carpettes, presumably after Ike Turner's Ikettes or Ray Charles' Raelettes.

'(Want You) Back In My Life Again' (Kerry Chater, Chris Christian)
Single A-side b/w 'Somebody's Been Lyin''
Release date: 28 August 1981
Charts: US: 72

A co-writer of this synth-led pop song was Kerry Chater – former member of Gary Puckett & the Union Gap, and occasional writing partner of John Bettis. The other writer, Chris Christian, had songs covered by Elvis Presley, Olivia Newton-John and Hall & Oates.

Richard has described how every effort was made to create a hit single, inviting Daryl Dragon (the Captain in Captain & Tennille) and Ian Underwood (formerly of Frank Zappa's Mothers of Invention) to programme the synthesizer sounds. Karen aims for a contemporary vocal sound, keeping it light and succinct. There's also a perky sax solo, string and harp parts and a moment towards the end where the backing vocals create a 16-voice multi-note chord on the word 'life'.

The single reached 72 in October. The band appeared on *The Merv Griffin Show* just as the single reached its peak, miming to the song and being interviewed with the other guests John Travolta and Karen's friend Olivia Newton-John.

'When You've Got What It Takes' (Roger Nichols, Bill Lane)
One of the album's lighter moments, this gentle number was written by former Paul Williams partner Roger Nichols with Bill Lane. The pair also wrote Paul Anka's 1976 hit 'Times of Your Life'.

The song features the gentle Latin rhythm of percussionist Paulinho DaCosta, and drummer John Robinson, who'd played on recent hits by The Brothers Johnson, George Benson and Michael Jackson. Karen's vocal is bright and confident to match the motivational lyric. Some fans are less enthusiastic about the track, and consider it to resemble a TV jingle.

'Somebody's Been Lying' (Carole Bayer Sager, Burt Bacharach)
The first Bacharach composition on a Carpenters' album since 1970's *Close To You* was written with his soon-to-be wife Carole Bayer Sager. She issued her own version of the song in 1981 on *Sometimes Late at Night*: a concept album following the ups and downs of a relationship, and Paulinho da Costa, Tim May and Fred Tackett play on both Sager's and the Carpenters' album.

This breakup song has a subtle theatricality, and Karen gives an understated, tremulous performance with mixed emotions alternating between tenderness and regret. Bacharach's sophisticated composition contains some intentionally out-of-place elements, like the bar of 2/4 at the start of Karen's second line that's followed immediately by an unsettling major-2nd chord, creating musical and thematic tension. Richard's intricate arrangement begins and ends with a dialogue between accusing wind and sheepish pizzicato strings. The final minute is wholly instrumental, dropping down to solo piano before rising to a concerto-like climax of emotional turmoil.

'I Believe You' (Dick Addrisi, Don Addrisi)
Single A-side b/w 'B'wana She No Home'
Release date: 20 October 1978
Charts: US: 68
This powerful ballad was written by The Addrisi brothers, best known for 'Never My Love': a hit for The Association, The 5th Dimension and Blue Swede. The first to have a hit with it was Dorothy Moore, who in 1977 reached 30 in the US and Canada, and 20 in the UK. Country artist Barbara Mandrell also recorded it on her September 1978 album *Moods*, one month before the Carpenters' single was released.

The Carpenters' recording reverses verses three and four, also changing the description of the little girl to 'freckled' instead of 'brown-eyed' in Moore's version and 'blue-eyed' in Mandrell's. The song deserved to be a bigger hit, not least for Karen's sincere and heartfelt interpretation of the romantic lyric, and for the stirring arrangement by Paul Riser, who worked on such legendary Motown releases as The Temptations' 'My Girl' and Marvin Gaye's 'I Heard It Through the Grapevine'.

'Touch Me When We're Dancing' (Kenny Bell, Terry Skinner, Jerry Lee Wallace)

Single A-side b/w 'Because We Are in Love (The Wedding Song)'
Release date: 19 June 1981
Charts: US: 16

This laid-back number was written and released by the group Bama in 1979, reaching 86. It saw greater success in 1986 as a Country number one for the similarly named Alabama.

The Carpenters extend their usual musical palette by adding electric sitar on the introduction, and a light soul groove. Karen sounds sultry, and session singer Carolyn Dennis joins the duo on backing vocals. Richard has acclaimed the track as 'one of our finest productions'.

Their first single since 1978, it went to 16, becoming their final top-20 hit. The video showed the band performing on the Chaplin stage at A&M, with superimposed footage of a couple dancing, and Bob Messenger playing the saxophone solo.

'When It's Gone (It's Just Gone)' (Randy Handley)

Written by Tennessee blues singer Randy Handley, this smooth country song was first covered by country star Charlie Rich in 1980. The Carpenters' recording features a heartbreaking vocal and a desolate, empty arrangement, haunted by spectral pedal steel playing from Jay Dee Maness.

Karen plays drums and percussion on the track with Larrie Londin and Bob Conti, respectively. Conti was a session player who'd previously worked with José Feliciano, Donna Summer and Wilson Pickett.

'Beechwood 4-5789' (Marvin Gaye, George Gordy, William 'Mickey' Stevenson)

Single A-side b/w 'Two Sides'
Release date: 2 March 1982
Charts: US: 74, UK: 78

The album's final single was the 1962 Motown golden oldie originally by The Marvelettes, (whose 'Please Mr. Postman' gave the Carpenters their third and final US number one in 1974). It was Karen's idea to record the catchy song and issue it as a single, which was released on her 32nd birthday. It was the last Carpenters single released during her lifetime.

The title refers to a phone number in the Beechwood district of Michigan. The nostalgic video shows 1960s teenagers dancing in a malt shop and then in miniature on a bedroom dressing table, as per the video effects of the day, all filmed on the Chaplin stage at A&M.

Karen's vocal is lively and vivacious, and the Latin-influenced rhythm was created by castanets and raked guitar strings, just as their last two 1960s covers had been ('There's A Kind Of Hush' and 'Breaking Up is Hard to Do'). Richard was pleased with the production, but later commented that they'd probably released enough golden oldies by this point, and should've been focussing on newer material. As it happened, the single reached only 74 in the US, though many other artists were having international top-10 hits with golden oldies at this time, such as Diana Ross with 'Why Do Fools Fall in Love?' (originally from 1956) and A Taste of Honey with 'Sukiyaki' (originally 1961).

'Because We Are In Love (The Wedding Song)' (Richard Carpenter, John Bettis)

Carpenter and Bettis wrote this song at Karen's request for her wedding to Tom Burris. It was completed just five days before the ceremony and was played as Karen walked down the aisle in the Crystal Room at the Beverly Hills Hotel on 31 August 1980.

Written in the style of Broadway standards, this deeply romantic song has an opening verse that is heard just once at the beginning. The lyrics eavesdrop on a conversation between a mother and an anxious bride-to-be seeking guidance on the morning of her wedding. Karen sounds childlike and vulnerable on lines like 'But I love him so', singing some of the highest notes of a melody that covers almost two octaves. Peter Knight's orchestration is rich and lush, while the O.K. Chorale vocal choir conducted by Frank Pooler supplies comforting, nostalgic tones.

Related Tracks
'Rainbow Connection' (Paul Williams, Kenny Ascher)

This wistful song was written for Kermit the Frog to sing in the opening scene of *The Muppet Movie* (1979). Williams and Ascher (the latter who previously worked on arrangements for John Lennon's solo albums and Meatloaf's *Bat Out of Hell*) also wrote songs for the 1976 Barbra Streisand film *A Star is Born*.

Richard's arrangement retains details from the soundtrack recording, such as the banjo-led country waltz, to which he added new elements – like the toy piano in the intro and recorder in the outro – and adjusted the chords. He also straightened out the melody's unusual flow – originally designed for the quirky speech patterns of the Kermit the Frog character – most notably on the opening lines.

The track was recorded in October 1980 during the *Made In America* sessions but remained in the can until 2001, when it was added to the *As Time Goes By* compilation at the request of fans. It was also released as a single in Japan, reaching number 47. Judy Collins and Mary O'Hara are two artists who have recorded the song.

By coincidence, just before this was finally released in 2001, The Jim Henson Company took over the vacated A&M lot in Hollywood: the site where the Carpenters recorded this song.

'The Uninvited Guest' (Buddy Kaye, Jeffrey M. Tweel)

This achingly sad tale of a woman coming to terms with her partner's affair was recorded in 1980 for *Made In America*. But the album already had the similar 'Strength of a Woman', which may be why the release of 'The Uninvited Guest' was delayed until *Lovelines* in 1989.

Songwriter Buddy Kaye had previously written 'The Old Songs' (with David Pomeranz; recorded by Barry Manilow), and 'The Christmas Alphabet', performed by Karen and Kristy McNichol on the 1977 TV Special *The Carpenters at Christmas*. The other writer, Jeff Tweel, had written songs for Skeeter Davis, Billie Jo Spears, Kenny Rogers and other country stars.

Richard's arrangement is empty and spacious, placing Karen's poignant vocal centre-stage, with ghostly pedal-steel whispers. The 1976 Mary McGregor hit 'Torn Between Two Lovers' is mentioned in the lyric.

'Kiss Me The Way You Did Last Night' (Margaret Dorn, Lynda Lee Lawley)

This gentle ballad was a collaboration between Margaret Dorn – who later joined Manhattan Transfer – and Lynda Lee Lawley, who wrote songs for the 1970s group Exile with producers Mike Chapman and Nicky Chinn.

The rhythm tracks were recorded in 1980 during the *Made In America* sessions. Orchestration was added in 1983, suggesting the song may have been considered for *Voice Of The Heart*. However, there were technical mixing difficulties; however, a solution was finally found in time for inclusion on *Lovelines* in 1989.

Voice Of The Heart (1983)

Personnel:
Karen Carpenter: lead and backing vocals
Richard Carpenter: backing vocals, keyboards, arranger
Tim May, Tony Peluso, Fred Tackett, Dennis Budimir: guitars
Jay Dee Maness: pedal steel guitar
Earle Dumler: oboe, English horn
Tom Scott: flutes
Gayle Levant: harp
Joe Osborn, Chuck Del'Monico: bass
Sheridon Stokes: flute, recorders
Chuck Findley, Ron Gorow John Audino: flugelhorn
John Phillips: tenor saxophone
Ed Greene, Ron Tutt, Larrie Londin: drums
Paulinho da Costa, Peter Limonick: percussion
The O.K. Chorale: backing vocals
Ron Hicklin: choir director
Dick Bolk: choir conductor
Peter Knight: orchestration, arranger (10)
Shaun Furlong: synthesizer programming
Jimmy Getzoff: concertmaster
Produced by Richard Carpenter
Recorded at A&M Recording Studios
Engineered by Roger 'Mingo' Young and Robert De La Garza
Mixed at A&M Recording Studios, Capitol Recording Studios, The Village
Recorder
Mix engineer: Roger Young, Robert De La Garza, David Cole, Robin Laine
Special thanks to Ron Gorow, John Bettis, Roger Young, Don Hahn, Mimi
Thomas, all the guys in the shop: Ken, Gary, Bill, Karl, Werner Wolfen, Herb,
Jerry and the entire A&M family.
Release date: 17 October 1983
Label: A&M
Charts: US: 46, UK: 6
Running Time: 40:24

On 4 February 1983, Karen tragically passed away at the age of 32. The main
cause of death was heart failure, the result of her drastic dieting as a sufferer
of anorexia nervosa. Though, of course, a terribly sad time, Richard returned
to the studio less than two months later, unsure of what else he should do.

Voice Of The Heart was the first of three posthumous compilations with
previously unreleased material, followed by *Lovelines* (1989) and *As Time
Goes By* (2001). 'Now' and 'You're Enough' were recorded in April 1982 for
the planned follow-up to *Made In America,* before sessions were paused as
Karen received psychological treatment in New York. Another five tracks

were *Made In America* outtakes, the remaining three being unused tracks from 1976 and 1977.

Many of the recordings had been left unfinished, requiring orchestral and choral overdubs, which took place around March/April 1983. All lead vocals were guides. The one exception was 'Sailing on the Tide', which was fully completed in 1977. However, given the quality of Karen's performances, one would hardly notice that the majority were not final vocal takes. All the same, Richard was never fully comfortable releasing so many outtakes. A list titled 'Buried Treasure' citing additional unreleased tracks circulates online, though further releases of rarities seem highly unlikely given Richard's position and the loss of Carpenters tapes in the Universal Music fire of 2008.

The album's chart peak of 46 was the group's highest since *A Kind Of Hush* in 1976, staying on the charts for 19 weeks and reaching Gold status. Richard couldn't hear any obvious singles on the album, but two were chosen nonetheless.

The front-cover photo of Karen was taken by photographer Claude Mougin, who also took the photos on Karen's solo album (released in 1996). Richard's back-cover shot was taken by Larry Williams, who photographed Richard for his 1987 solo album *Time*. The inner sleeve used a shot by Annie Leibovitz from the duo's 1974 *Rolling Stone* interview.

'Now' (Roger Nichols, Dean Pitchford)

'Now' is a poignant love song that sets the tone for an album of mostly mid-tempo ballads. Co-writer Dean Pitchford also wrote the theme songs for the movies *Fame* (1980) and *Footloose* (1984).

'Now' has the feel of a classic stage show number, capturing the excitement and uncertainty of a new relationship. Given that this vocal was a guide, the performance is strong and nuanced, employing vibrato and other vocal techniques to skilfully interpret the lyric. Richard's arrangement ranges from small details (orchestrally illustrating the sound of wind and thunder in the opening verse) to dramatic moments like the chorus' surging choir lines. There's also a brief saxophone solo from John Phillips.

Recorded on 25 April 1982 at A&M Studio D, sadly, this was the last thing Karen recorded. The orchestra and choir parts were overdubbed in April 1983.

'Sailing On The Tide' (Tony Peluso, John Bettis)

This feel-good fantasy about fleeing to a boat in the Caribbean brings some sunshine to side one. Bettis and Peluso had previously collaborated on 'Happy' from 1975's *Horizon*. 'Sailing on the Tide' was written around the same time as 'Happy', and an early recording was never released. This later recording is from 1977.

Like 'Happy', 'Sailing on the Tide' has a breezy, cheerful arrangement, and Karen sounds similarly relaxed, stretching out on the word 'sunshine'. A false ending at the 3:30 mark goes into a coda section, featuring a bass solo from Joe Osborn and a woodwind part from Earle Dumler.

'You're Enough' (Richard Carpenter, John Bettis)

Like 'Now', this basic track and vocals were recorded in April 1982. Karen's vocal has all the conviction of a final performance. Richard's arrangement manages to be both contemporary and nostalgic, mixing electric guitar solos with 1940s-style choral accompaniment and diminished and augmented chords. An extra layer of sweetness is added with tinkling glockenspiels and childlike recorders played by Sheridon Stokes. There's also a faint musical echo of 'Close To You', coming from Richard's piano introduction and Chuck Findley's flugelhorn outro.

'Make Believe It's Your First Time' (Bob Morrison, Johnny Wilson)

Single A-side b/w 'Look to Your Dreams'
Release date: 4 October 1983
Charts: US: -, UK: 60

This tender love song was written by country songwriters Morrison and Wilson, who wrote for the likes of Kenny Rogers, Olivia Newton-John and Brenda Lee. Wilson had been a member of Roy Orbison's high school band, The Wink Westerners. The song was first released by Johnny Rodriguez in 1978, with another four versions (including one by Bobby Vinton) appearing before the Carpenters' single.

Karen first recorded this song during New York sessions for her unreleased solo album, with a piano arrangement similar to the Carpenters' style. Perhaps unsurprisingly, Richard thought the song might fit well on *Made In America*, and a rhythm track and vocal were recorded in October 1980. One significant change from Karen's solo album version was the writers' inclusion of a new bridge at Richard's request. The track was left unfinished until being reconsidered for *Voice Of The Heart,* with guitar parts added in March 1983, and orchestra and choir parts the following month.

An off-mic comment from Karen has been left at the start of the track: 'Ugh! I have to get into a serious mood here'. Then makes a tap-dancing noise by pulling her cheek three times: a Carpenters road-band in-joke. Following this, she gives a beautiful and sensuous rendition, concluding with a long, sustained note. The spoken introduction was removed when the track was issued in October 1983 as the album's first single.

'Two Lives' (Mark Terrence Jordan)

Previously recorded by Bonnie Raitt and Randy Crawford, this elegant ballad was written by Mark Jordan: a Nashville pianist who has played on albums by Van Morrison, Maria Muldaur and Leo Sayer. The Carpenters originally recorded their version in June 1980 for *Made In America*. When the track didn't make that album, it was polished up in April 1983, though the vocal part remains a guide. Karen's singing is captivating throughout, though Richard notes that she stood further from the microphone than usual, and the recording loses some presence as a result.

Richard's arrangement falls somewhere between country rock and a hymn, thanks to the church organ in the introduction and the solemn choral backing vocals. Aside from 'Prime Time Love', 'Two Lives' is the album's first in a sequence of breakup songs that conclude with 'Your Baby Doesn't Love You Anymore'.

'At The End Of A Song' (Richard Carpenter, John Bettis)
This laid-back song begins side two, and as the opening lines refer to travelling the world, the arrangement appears to do likewise, with marimba, recorder, Spanish guitar, pedal steel and harp all suggestive of a trip to far-away places.

Karen's interpretation of the lyric manages to balance weariness and hope, climbing up and plunging down on the chorus melody. This was another song originally considered for *Made In America*, with rhythm tracks and guide vocals recorded in November 1980. Further orchestration was added by Richard in early 1983.

'Ordinary Fool' (Paul Williams)
In 1976, it was four years since the duo had recorded a Paul Williams song. During sessions for *A Kind Of Hush,* they started work on this wistful ballad that Williams had just completed for the musical comedy *Bugsy Malone* released that summer.

The song segues seamlessly from the prior track, drifting between major and minor keys. Richard's arrangement conjures the jazz-like feel of the *Bugsy Malone* soundtrack, thanks in part to the double-bass playing of Chuck Domanico (listed here as Chuck Del'Monico): a legendary sideman to Frank Sinatra, Chet Baker and Henry Mancini. The arrangement is kept fairly sparse overall, with a light patina of strings and brass, and a bluesy saxophone solo from John Phillips.

A significant deviation from the *Bugsy Malone* version is that Karen sings the melody an octave lower than Julie McWhirter: the singing voice for the character Blousy Brown. McWhirter has also voiced the cartoon character Casper the Friendly Ghost, and is married to DJ Rick Dees. Ella Fitzgerald and Mel Tormé also recorded the song.

'Prime Time Love' (Mary Unobsky, Danny Ironstone)
This smooth R&B track was another originally considered for *Made In America,* contrasting with the *Voice Of The Heart* ballads. Unobsky and Ironstone had written songs for Rita Coolidge, and 'Prime Time Love' was previously recorded by English singer Jess Roden for his 1980 album *Stonechaser*.

Karen sounds relaxed and seductive, singing the slinky melody, while Richard supplies backing harmonies and delivers the immortal line 'That's a bummer'. The punchy brass, slick strings, Latin percussion and saxophone solo all add a touch of disco.

'Your Baby Doesn't Love You Anymore' (Larry Weiss)
Single A-side b/w 'Sailing on the Tide'
Release date: 31 January 1984
This golden oldie was a minor 1965 hit for Ruby and the Romantics, who'd also recorded 'Hurting Each Other'. Songwriter Larry Weiss also wrote 'Bend Me, Shape Me' for Amen Corner, 'Hi Ho, Silver Lining' for Jeff Beck, and 'Rhinestone Cowboy' for Glen Campbell. The title appears to borrow a phrase from the opening line of Roy Orbison's 1964 top-10 hit 'It's Over'.

The Carpenters first considered the song for *Made In America*, recording the rhythm track and vocal in October 1980, but ultimately selecting 'Beechwood 4-5789' instead. Over a repeated bass note, Karen lists a recipe for misery, as the melodramatic verse builds to a cathartic chorus. Though the single didn't reach the pop chart, it did hit 12 on *Billboard*'s Adult Contemporary chart.

'Look To Your Dreams' (Richard Carpenter, John Bettis)
This stirring Carpenter/Bettis song was written in 1974 at Karen's request for 'a cross between a standard and a show tune'. It remained unrecorded until late 1977, around the time of the *Christmas Portrait* sessions. Though Richard was reluctant to release it, Karen never forgot the song, and it was also said to have been their mother's favourite.

It begins with a flute line slightly reminiscent of Henry Mancini's 'Moon River', before Karen sings an introductory verse written in imitation of standards like 'Nice Work If You Can Get It' or 'Let's Call the Whole Thing Off'. The lyric urges us to remember our dreams and desires, offering the insight 'Fantasy's reality's childhood'. The distant piano coda is a moving and dignified tribute to Karen's memory but was removed when the track was issued as the B-side to 'Make Believe It's Your First Time'.

An Old-Fashioned Christmas (1984)

Personnel:
Richard Carpenter: vocals, arrangements, keyboards
Karen Carpenter: vocals
Pete Jolly: keyboards
Skiala Kanga, Gayle Levant: harp
Peter Knight: arrangement (2-9, 12-14)
Billy May: arrangement (10)
Barry Morgan, Ron Tutt: drums
Joe Osborn: bass
Pete Morgan: upright bass
The O.K. Chorale: Dick Bolks
English Choir: background vocals – Director/Conductor: Robert Howes
John 'Francis' Phillips: Tenor saxophone
Richard Carpenter: producer
Karen Carpenter, Jack Daugherty: producers (11)
Recorded at A&M, Hollywood, CA; EMI Abbey Road Studios, London, UK
Eric Tomlinson, Alan Rouse, Robert De La Garza, Ray Gerhardt, Roger Young: Engineers
John Richards, Roger Young: Mixing
Release date: 26 October 1984
Label: A&M
Charts: US: 190, UK: -
Running Time 48:45

Karen and Richard were both big fans of Christmas music, but when the idea for a Carpenters Christmas album was proposed in the early days of their career, A&M were unenthusiastic, considering Christmas albums to be corny and out-of-date. Indifference changed to concern when the costs of recording an orchestra and choir turned *Christmas Portrait* into the duo's most expensive album to that point. However, the project's eventual success not only allayed label fears, but led to a request for a second Christmas album, drawing on numerous outtakes from the first. Of these, only seven featured Karen, so arranger/conductor Peter Knight, a 70-piece orchestra and the O.K. Chorale choir all joined Beatles fan Richard at London's Abbey Road Studios to embellish Karen's recordings and furnish a full album of Christmas classics.

Though only reaching 190 in the US, the album was eventually certified Gold. For the cover, Robert Tannenbaum created another Norman Rockwell-style portrait of Karen and Richard, with Santa, elves, and assorted toys, including a nutcracker soldier.

'It Came Upon a Midnight Clear' (Edmund Sears, Richard Storrs Willis)
Like *Christmas Portrait*, the album opens with an *a cappella* arrangement of a well-known carol. American Unitarian minister Edmund Sears first wrote

the words as a poem in 1849, with American composer Willis setting it to music in 1850.

This cheerful carol has a lilting 6/8 metre, delivered in a jazz-like style reminiscent of The Beach Boys. Richard recorded the nine-part vocal arrangement in Studio D at A&M before heading to Abbey Road Studios to continue work on the album.

'Overture'
A. 'Happy Holiday' (Irving Berlin)
B. 'The First Noel' (Trad. Old English Carol, arr. Richard Carpenter)
C. 'March Of The Toys' (Victor Herbert)
D. 'Little Jesus' (Trad. Czech carol, Trans. Percy Dearmer, Arr. Richard Carpenter)
E. 'I Saw Mommy Kissing Santa Claus' (Tommie Connor)
F. 'O Little Town Of Bethlehem' (Phillips Brooks, L. H. Redner)
G. 'In Dulce Jubilo' (14th-century German melody)
H. 'Gesu Bambino' (The Infant Jesus) (Pietro A. Yon)
I. 'Angels We Have Heard On High' (Trad. French carol, James Chadwick)

The overture begins with the O.K. Chorale singing 'Happy Holiday' – a jolly affirmation of the season, written in 1942 for the Bing Crosby film *Holiday Inn,* which also included 'White Christmas'. Richard and the choir then sing 'The First Noel', a traditional English carol first collected and published in the 1820s.

Next, military drums and trumpets muster us for the album's first instrumental – the bright and lively 'March of the Toys', composed for the operetta *Babes in Toyland* by American Victor Herbert. This Broadway show was adapted into a 1930s Christmas film starring Laurel and Hardy, and again by Disney in the 1960s. The operetta also includes the song 'Toyland', which Perry Como sang in his 1974 Christmas TV special that had the Carpenters as guests.

'Little Jesus' or 'Rocking Song' is a lullaby from a Czech carol, included in the *Oxford Book of Carols* in 1928. The O.K. Chorale sing it here in a near *a cappella*.

Next is the lighthearted 'I Saw Mommy Kissing Santa Claus', commissioned in 1952 by the New York department store Saks to promote their Christmas card design. An accompanying recording by 13-year-old singer Jimmy Boyd reached number 1. Spike Jones issued a version soon after, though his was less successful. The song was written by Englishman Tommie Connor, who wrote comic tunes like 'The Biggest Aspidistra in the World' for Gracie Fields, and 'Never Tango with an Eskimo' for Alma Cogan. Here, Peter Knight created a gently swinging arrangement, passing the melody between vibraphone, muted trumpet and strings.

The remaining selections are all religious carols, beginning with Richard's rendition of 'O Little Town of Bethlehem'. The words come from a 19th-century poem by American Episcopal clergyman Phillips Brooks, and this recording uses the melody line that's most familiar in the U.S.

The next piece is an instrumental excerpt from 'In Dulce Jubilo' – a German carol from the Middle Ages which is often accompanied by the lyric 'Good Christian Men, Rejoice'. This piece segues into the instrumental 'Gesu Bambino': a carol from 1917 written by the Italian Pietro Yon. The overture climaxes with the O.K. Chorale singing 'Angels We Have Heard On High' – a 19th-century English adaptation of a French carol. A gentle orchestral segue then leads into the album's title track.

'An Old-Fashioned Christmas' (Richard Carpenter, John Bettis)
Carpenter and Bettis wrote this especially for the album. Richard sings with the O.K. Chorale. Starting with a group of female voices and electric piano, further orchestral elements are added throughout, although the arrangement never becomes too dense, and it instils a sense of wonder.

'O Holy Night' (Adolphe Adam, Adapted by Richard Carpenter)
A segue links the previous song to this 19th-century religious poem written by French poet Placide Cappeau and set to music by French composer Adolphe Adam. Richard played this on the piano with orchestra and choir on the 1977 TV special *The Carpenters at Christmas*. A new orchestral arrangement was recorded for *Christmas Portrait,* but when the song was dropped from that album, Karen didn't record a vocal. Therefore, the melody has been shared between choir and piano. Richard's dramatic piano solo is one of the album's most dramatic moments.

'(There's No Place Like) Home For The Holidays' (Robert Allen, Al Stillman)
Karen's first appearance on this album is on this song originally written for Perry Como and also recorded by Bobby Vee, Jim Nabors and Engelbert Humperdinck. Karen's warm and friendly vocal was recorded in February 1978. Richard sang the song on the 1984 Christmas edition of the chart show *Solid Gold,* which also featured Barry Manilow, Anne Murray, Suzanne Somers and John Davidson.

'Medley'
A. 'Here Comes Santa Claus' (Gene Autry, Oakley Haldeman)
B. 'Frosty The Snowman' (Steve Nelson, Jack Rollins)
C. 'Rudolph The Red-Nosed Reindeer' (Johnny Marks)
D. 'Good King Wenceslas' (John Mason Neale, Adapted by Richard Carpenter)
For this upbeat piano-led instrumental medley, Peter Knight and Richard combined three popular children's Christmas songs from the 1940s and 1950s with a traditional 19th-century carol.

The three children's songs had been made famous by cowboy movie star Gene Autry, and had also appeared on Spike Jones' 1956 album *Xmas Spectacular.*

The medley begins with 'Here Comes Santa Claus'. Autry had the idea for the lyric when leading the 1946 Santa Claus Lane Parade, now known as the Hollywood Christmas Parade. The crowds chanted, 'Here Comes Santa Claus!', and by the following year, Autry had turned his idea into a top-10 hit. He did it again in 1950 with 'Frosty the Snowman', which tells the story of a snowman who magically comes to life after children place a hat on his head. Autry's original ends with the coda 'Thumpity thump thump, Thumpity thump thump, Look at Frosty go, Over the hills of snow', which Knight turns into a segue into 'Rudolph the Red-Nosed Reindeer'. That song was Autry's biggest Christmas hit, going to number one in 1950, and selling 25,000,000 copies.

Completing the medley is 'Good King Wenceslas', the words of which were adapted from a Czech poem by English hymn writer John Mason Neale in 1853, and set to the 13th-century Spring carol 'Eastertime Has Come'. Peter Knight's arrangement switches between brass band and jazz trio settings.

'Little Altar Boy' (Howlett Peter Smith)
The mood turns reflective for Karen's second appearance. This 1961 song was originally recorded by Vic Dana, while Andy Williams, Glen Campbell and Jack Jones all included it on their 1960s Christmas albums.

Karen's captivating interpretation was recorded in February 1978, and with Peter Knight's gentle arrangement, it makes for a stunning experience. It is so stunning that Richard considers this to be his favourite performance by Karen. In late 1984, the track was issued as a promo single backed with 'Do You Hear What I Hear?'.

'Do You Hear What I Hear?' (Noël Regney, Gloria Shayne)
This husband-and-wife songwriting team wrote this appeal for peace in 1962 during the Cuban Missile Crisis. The song was a hit for The Harry Simeone Chorale, and was recorded by Bing Crosby and at least 500 other artists since.

Karen recorded a guide vocal in December 1977, but apparently was distracted at the beginning, mumbling the first two lines. For its 1984 release, Richard sang that verse, though the choir can be heard singing the wrong responses, as 'Do you see what I see?' is answered with 'Do you hear what I hear?', a mistake in the choir part that Richard did not get around to repairing, according to Lennox and May's book.

The arrangement builds steadily throughout, modulating upwards through two keys to a climax where Karen holds her final note for four bars.

'My Favorite Things' (Richard Rodgers, Oscar Hammerstein II)
Following the success of Rodgers and Hammerstein's 1959 Broadway musical *The Sound of Music,* this song became a popular jazz standard, with recordings by Sarah Vaughn, Mark Murphy, saxophonist John Coltrane and many others. Once Jones included this non-seasonal song on a Christmas

album in 1964, other artists did the same, including The Supremes, Andy Williams and Herb Alpert. Here, Peter Knight creates a playful waltz arrangement for piano, orchestra and choir.

'He Came Here For Me' (Ron Nelson)

American composer Ron Nelson wrote this religious anthem in 1960 as a choral piece. The dramatic arrangement of this version is by Billy May, with Karen leading the choir, again demonstrating the stylistic versatility of her voice on this sombre hymn.

'Santa Claus Is Coming To Town' (Haven Gillespie, John Frederick Coots)

Unlike the upbeat *Christmas Portrait* version, this is the ballad version featuring Karen that was first released as a single in 1974. The track was remixed for this album with a new saxophone solo. A full discussion of this song can be found in the Related Tracks section following the album *Now And Then*.

'What Are You Doing New Year's Eve?' (Frank Loesser)

This poignant 1947 ballad comes from masterly songwriter Frank Loesser, who wrote the musicals *Guys and Dolls* and *Hans Christian Andersen* and wrote the lyrics for Hoagy Carmichael's 'Heart and Soul' and 'Two Sleepy People'.

'What Are You Doing New Year's Eve?' was a Christmas hit for The Orioles in 1949, though Loesser's daughter, writing in 2000, points out that it's not strictly a Christmas song, and that the lyric merely depicts someone 'madly in love, making a (possibly rash) commitment far into the future', as shown in the opening lines 'Maybe it's much too early in the game/But I thought I'd ask you just the same'. Nevertheless, the song has been included on a host of Christmas albums, including Spike Jones' *Xmas Spectacular,* where the song ended with a quote from 'Auld Lang Syne', as does this version. Here, Peter Knight created a laid-back jazz arrangement for Karen to demonstrate how well-suited she was to jazz standards.

'Selections from The Nutcracker' (Pyotr Ilyich Tchaikovsky)
A. 'Overture Miniature'
B. 'Dance Of The Sugar Plum Fairy'
C. 'Trepak'
D. 'Valse Des Fleurs'

Tchaikovsky's ever-popular Christmas-themed *Nutcracker* ballet dates from 1892, with a magical fantasy plot based on German author E. T. A. Hoffman's short story *The Nutcracker and the Mouse King*. Its inclusion on this album gave Richard the opportunity to play both the piano and the chiming celesta for 'Dance of the Sugar Plum Fairy'. 'Trepak' is a high-spirited and energetic

Ukrainian folk dance, while 'Valse des Fleurs' sees flowers magically come to life and dance at the bidding of the fairy.

'I Heard The Bells On Christmas Day' (Johnny Marks, Henry Wadsworth Longfellow)
The album ends with a Christmas poem written by American poet Longfellow in 1863 during the American Civil War. The narrator despairs that though Christmas bells are ringing, there's little hope for mankind, given their inclination to fight:

And in despair I bowed my head
'There is no peace on earth', I said

Luckily, by the poem's end, his faith in humanity is restored:

The Wrong shall fail, the Right prevail

These words have been set to many different melodies, this one by Johnny Marks, who wrote 'Rudolph the Red-Nosed Reindeer', 'Rockin' Around the Christmas Tree' and 'An Old-Fashioned Christmas'.

The Carpenters' version was recorded in December 1977. Karen sounds especially solemn as she reaches down to a low E on the second line. The turning of a page can be heard unintentionally at the end of verse one, whereas the very much intended sound of tubular bells can be heard in the final verse and on the final line, 'With peace on Earth, goodwill to men'.

Live Albums And Bootlegs

Live In Japan (1975)

Release date: March 1975
Label: King Records

Two live albums were released in the 1970s: *Live in Japan* and *Live at the Palladium*. *Live in Japan* was from three nights in June 1974 at the Festival Hall in Osaka. The album reached number eight in Japan and became available as an import in other countries.

The set opens with a medley of 'Superstar', 'Rainy Days And Mondays' and 'Goodbye To Love', and includes other hits, album tracks and the oldies medley. In addition to three of the oldies from *Now And Then*, the set also includes classics like The Beach Boys' 'Little Honda', Del Shannon's 'Runaway', The Shangri-Las' 'Leader of the Pack', The Monotones' 'The Book of Love', The Chords' 'Sh-Boom', Shep and the Limelites' 'Daddy's Home' and Chuck Berry's 'Johnny B. Goode'. A brief burst of the 'Colonel Bogey March' – a well-known piece from 1914 – is played as the Kyoto Children's Choir arrive onstage to perform 'Sing'. Having previously recorded a Spanish version, Karen also learnt a Japanese translation of the song, which she performs here.

The Carpenters-produced double album came in a gatefold sleeve with a lyric booklet and photos stapled inside, and a poster of the pair in traditional Japanese clothing. The players were their established touring band of Tony Peluso, Bob Messenger, Doug Strawn, Danny Woodhams and Cubby O'Brien, with Karen playing drums on 'Help', 'Mr. Guder', 'Da Doo Ron Ron' and 'Johnny B. Goode'. Richard sings lead on 'Little Honda', 'The Book of Love' and 'Daddy's Home', with 'Runaway' and 'Sh-Boom sung by Pete Henderson: half of their comedy opening act Skiles and Henderson.

Aside from a few additions and omissions, the album sequence was almost identical to the concert filmed for Japanese NTV at Tokyo's Budokan arena a week earlier, on 31 May. The Budokan concert was released on laserdisc in 1996 by Polygram Video, and on VHS by A&M, with a DVD following in 2001. In 2020, Stiletto Discs issued a digital audio-only version on streaming sites titled *The Road to Yesterday*.

Live At The Palladium (1976)

Release date: December 1976
Label: A&M, reissued in the UK on Pickwick
UK: 28

In November 1976, the Carpenters made their first UK appearances since 1974, to promote their seventh album, *A Kind Of Hush*. The tour included Edinburgh, Manchester, Blackpool and Birmingham, before dates at London's historic Palladium theatre from November 22nd to 27th. They conclude the trip by filming an *In Concert* BBC TV special at the New London Theatre on 28 November. The Palladium was built in 1910, and hosted shows by Louis

Armstrong, Judy Garland, Frank Sinatra and Josephine Baker. The Beatles' October 1963 performance there for ITV's *Sunday Night at the Palladium* launched Beatlemania in the UK.

The band is the same as on *Live in Japan*, accompanied by an orchestra conducted by American Dick Palombi, who later worked for Neil Sedaka. The set begins with an upbeat and updated version of 'Flat Baroque', providing a showcase for Richard and the band. Karen then arrives to sing their recent hit 'There's A Kind Of Hush (All Over The World)' and 'Jambalaya (On the Bayou)'. Next, Richard sings 'Piano Picker', with new lyrics telling the duo's story. During the song, Karen reappears to play drums, leading into an energetic drum solo on a medley of Gershwin numbers. Richard and the orchestra then perform the 'Warsaw Concerto', side one concluding with Cole Porter's 'From This Moment On'. For that tune, Karen sings while Richard plays Bach's 'Prelude No. 2' from *The Well Tempered Clavier*. This combination was the idea of Ken and Mitzie Welch: the husband-and-wife team who'd redesigned the stage show and had also worked with Barbra Streisand, Burt Bacharach, Barry Manilow and comedian Carol Burnett.

Side two features a medley of ten of their biggest singles, ending with 'We've Only Just Begun'. Numbers from the concert that *didn't* make the album, included 'I Need to Be in Love', 'Sing' (with audience interaction), 'Close To You' sung by Richard in a Spike Jones comedy style, 'Yesterday Once More' leading into a medley of songs from the stage musical *Grease*, and an encore that interpolated 'Coming Through the Rye' with 'Good Vibrations'. Several of these numbers can be found in three filmed concerts from 1976 – the first at the Osaka Festival Hall in March, the second in Amsterdam on 14 November, and the last filmed by the BBC at the New London Theatre on 28 November.

The album reached 24 in Japan, and 28 in the UK, where it went gold. Though not released in the US, copies were available on import. The duo produced the album, which was mixed and mastered in London. No singles were issued.

Bootlegs

There are plenty of Carpenters' live bootleg CDs and DVDs in circulation, many from live radio and TV broadcasts. For instance, the audio from the 1971 *Live at the BBC* TV special of studio appearances has been repackaged as *The Carpenters Live on Stage* (Immortal), and incorrectly as *Live in New York 1971* by Japanese bootleg label Alive the Live. This CD also includes two short European sets from February 1974 – the first from Amsterdam as broadcast by AVRO-TV, and the second from Hasselt, Belgium. The same label also issued *Live in Japan 1972* – a radio broadcast from Japan's NHK network, live from the Budokan in Tokyo. This CD also includes the May 1971 concert at New York's Carnegie Hall, as broadcast by NHK's BS2 channel.

The DVD *Carpenters – From Down Under to Far East* (Footstomp) is a concert from the May 8-20 1972 residency at Sydney's Chevron Hotel, broadcast in black-and-white by Australia's 7 network.

A VPRO broadcast of a November 1976 concert at the Jaap Eden Hall in Amsterdam has appeared under several titles, such as *The Carpenters – Live in Amsterdam 1976* (No label), *Carpenters – Live at the Amsterdam* (poisonAPPLE) and *Holding Onto Yesterday (Live 1976)* (Firefly).

Several further CDs collate radio interviews, studio outtakes and so forth, and there are DVDs collecting various TV appearances and adverts. The quality of these bootlegs is hit-and-miss, though many have been uploaded to YouTube or specialised fan sites.

Compilations And Tribute Albums

Over 50 compilations released since 1971 are proof of the band's enduring popularity. Due to the sheer quantity, I have focussed on the best sellers and those that offered something new. I've selected three high-profile tribute albums, but have avoided the many soundalike or instrumental budget-label releases from the 1970s and 1980s.

While some compilations focus on the best-known hits, others feature rare and previously unreleased material, as discussed in the Related Tracks sections of this book. For certain key compilations, Richard has used revisited and remixed tracks, enhancing the sound quality and addressing audio problems found in the original recordings.

The first compilations appeared overseas, with five issued in Japan alone between 1971 and 1973, including the first two double albums in the *Gem Of* series. The 1972 compilation *Great Hits of The Carpenters* was the first to be issued in Australasia.

The Singles 1969-1973 (1973)

This first international compilation appeared in December 1973 at the height of the band's chart success. Richard wanted a title different to the generic *Greatest Hits*, which he felt was often misused when acts had only scored a couple of hits and padded out their albums with filler.

This compilation contained 12 singles, skipping 'Bless the Beasts and Children' and 'Merry Christmas, Darling'. Maintaining the duo's tradition of album bookends, it begins and ends with 'Close To You', heard at the start in a miniature overture with a theme based on 'Superstar', and in full as the closing track. 'Top Of The World' was issued as a single to coincide with the compilation's release, and includes several re-recorded parts, such as the pedal steel, additional guitar fills, Richard's Wurlitzer electric piano and Karen's vocal, since she was never happy with her original performance. 'Ticket To Ride' similarly features new drums, piano and guitar tracks, as well as a new vocal from Karen.

The French horn part on the introduction to 'Superstar' has an extra chord at the end, while the song itself has an extra chord played by the strings and harp to segue into 'Rainy Days And Mondays'. Richard originally intended to link these two songs on the *Carpenters* (Tan) album, but on account of how strong they both were, Richard agreed to Herb Alpert's suggestion of making them opening tracks on each side. 'Rainy Days And Mondays' then links into 'Goodbye To Love', and both are slightly sped up: a decision Richard later regretted.

The album appeared in a brown gatefold sleeve with gold lettering, echoing the prominent band logo on the *Carpenters* (Tan) and *A Song For You* covers. Inside was a sepia picture of the duo, and a booklet with liner notes by journalist Digby Diehl. The collection proved to be extremely popular, receiving positive reviews in *Billboard*, *Record World* and *Rolling Stone*. It went seven times multi-platinum in the US, though it was their only number-one album there. In the UK, it stayed at number one for 17 weeks, placing it at number six in the UK's top-10 highest-selling albums of the 1970s – alongside *Abba's Greatest Hits*, Mike Oldfield's *Tubular Bells* and Pink Floyd's *Dark Side of the Moon*.

The Singles 1974-1978 (1978)
In late 1978, this compilation was issued in the UK, Canada and Japan, though not in the US, due to a decline in the band's popularity there. It fared well in the UK, spending three weeks at number two, and going platinum, thanks no doubt to extensive advertising. Karen also made a solo visit to London, performing two songs on the *Bruce Forsyth's Big Night* TV show, and signing records at Chappell's music store in Bond Street.

The album was packaged in a shiny gold metallic sleeve, embossed with an art deco design depicting a sunrise. The album contained 12 songs, including the B-sides 'Happy' and 'Can't Smile Without You'. The A-sides 'Santa Claus Is Comin' to Town', 'Goofus' and the Japanese single 'Breaking Up Is Hard to Do' were left out. Some tracks were the single edits.

Yesterday Once More (1984, 1985)
This was available initially as a double vinyl album or two-cassette package via TV mail order. In 1985, it was released on vinyl, CD, cassette and 8-track, with an expanded tracklist and eight remixes. The album reached 10 in the UK, but stuck at 144 on the *Billboard* 200.

The album includes the versions of 'Superstar'/'Rainy Days And Mondays' and 'Goodbye To Love' from *The Singles 1969-1973* compilation, except they were slowed back down to their original speed. A greatest hits video collection of the same title was released on VHS and Betamax in 1985.

Anthology (1985), Treasures (1987), A&M Composer Series (1988)
Also appearing in 1985 was the four-LP set *Anthology*, in Japan only. This was the biggest collection to date, featuring many remixes and the first release of 'Honolulu City Lights'. It also included the full-length Bacharach/David medley, recorded live at the Riviera Motel in May 1974. Another feature of *Anthology* was that the tracks smoothly segued from one to the next, with many songs slightly sped up or down to match one another. The compilation was reissued on four CDs in 1989, and again in 1997, with a few track changes and mostly using the latest remixes.

In 1987 came the Japanese release *Treasures*. This two-CD set was arranged chronologically and focussed mainly on album tracks. Uniquely, it included two 1985 remixes and a further nine from 1987. Several of these include new piano and keyboard parts, and haven't appeared on any other release. This was also the first release of 'Slow Dance', ahead of its inclusion on *Lovelines* in 1989.

In 1988, three volumes of the Japanese *A&M Composers Series* were issued, the second focusing on Carpenter/Bettis songs, with sixteen Carpenters' recordings and 'I'm Still Not Over You' from Richard's 1987 solo album *Time*. The first and third volumes concentrated on Bacharach/David and Williams/Nichols songs, respectively. The similar collection *Carpenters Perform Carpenter* came out in 2003, and included 'Karen's Theme' from Richard's second solo album *Richard Carpenter: Pianist, Arranger, Composer, Conductor* (1998).

Lovelines (1989)

The CBS-TV production *The Karen Carpenter Story* premiered on 1 January 1989, with Cynthia Gibb playing the role of Karen. The TV drama received record ratings, and sparked renewed interest in the band's music, with a 400% increase in sales over the ensuing weeks. The movie featured the previously unheard tracks 'You're the One' and 'Where Do I Go From Here?'. While there was no soundtrack album, the *Lovelines* compilation appeared in October 1989, marking the 20th anniversary of the band signing to A&M.

Spanning the period 1977 to 1980, the tracks comprised outtakes from albums and TV specials, and four songs from Karen's then-unheard solo album. 'Little Girl Blue' was featured in the 1978 TV special *The Carpenters... Space Encounters*, and 'Honolulu City Lights' had been recorded between albums in 1978. That track was issued as a single in 1986, but failed to chart. 'If I Had You' came from Karen's unreleased solo album, and was issued as a single in November 1989, reaching 18 on the Adult Contemporary chart.

Though it's a set of outtakes, the collection is often seen as the final Carpenters studio album, and the production and sequencing give it an overall feeling of coherence. *Lovelines* was included with all of the studio albums in the 1989 limited-edition 12-CD box set *The Compact Disc Collection*. Both of the Christmas albums were combined into a single disc for this set. Discussions of the songs on that album can be found in the Related Tracks sections of earlier chapters.

Only Yesterday – Their Greatest Hits (1990)

This 20-song single CD compilation was released in the US as *Their Greatest Hits*. Though it failed to chart there, it became a multi-platinum seller around the world, going to number one in the UK and New Zealand for seven weeks, and Ireland for one week.

From The Top (1991)/The Essential Collection: 1965-1997 (2002)

Further rarities were issued in the 4-CD 1991 box set *From the Top*. Spanning the years 1965 to 1982, it was initially packaged as a 12-inch set holding the CDs in individual jewel cases, then was redesigned as a slim book with the discs attached at the back. Both versions came with liner notes from Richard. Highlights include their earliest ventures, such as a rehearsal recording of the

Richard Carpenter Trio, Karen's 1960s Magic Lamp solo singles, and demos by The Summerchimes and Spectrum.

   Also of interest are studio outtakes, a radio interview, songs from the TV specials, and TV jingles for Japanese soft drinks and the AT&T telephone company. 40 of the 67 tracks were remixes, and 20 were previously unreleased. The set was revised in 2002 and re-released under the title *The Essential Collection: 1965-1997*. This issue added 18 tracks, including another Japanese TV jingle. This compilation focused more on the hits, and a few tracks from the first compilation were removed to make way for better-known songs. The final track was 'Karen's Theme' – released as a single in 1997, and included on Richard's second solo album.

Best Of Best + / Original Master Karaoke – Yesterday Once More (1992)
Fans in Japan – the country that gave the world karaoke – naturally demanded karaoke versions of the Carpenters' songs, and Richard was keen to see that the band's music was represented properly. 15 songs from 1970-1976 were selected for a CD of original recordings, and a second CD of karaoke versions. To create these, he remixed the tracks without Karen's vocals. The disc was very popular and was reissued in 1994 and again in 2005, with the addition of 'Sing'.

Interpretations (1994)
Throughout the early 1990s, compilations continued apace, including six themed CDs in Japan's *Sweet Memory* series. They utilised many of the remixes, though the only exclusive track was a remix of 'Another Song' (from 1970's *Close To You*) with new bass from Joe Osborn.

   The next major A&M compilation was *Interpretations*, released in 1994 to mark the 25th anniversary of the first Carpenters album *Offering*. This themed compilation collated 21 Carpenters recordings by other songwriters. A 16-song version was released in the US the following year. Both versions included three previously unreleased tracks: 'Without a Song' from the 1980 TV special *Music, Music, Music*, 'From This Moment On' recorded for the same special but unused, and 'Tryin' to Get the Feeling Again': a 1975 *Horizon* outtake. A VHS, also entitled *Interpretations,* was released in 1995, mostly compiled from TV performances. This was re-released on DVD in 2003.

If I Were A Carpenter – Various Artists (1994)
The average Carpenters tribute album is typically filled with either soundalike remakes or easy-listening instrumentals, like *The Carpenters Song Book* by The Boston Pops Orchestra, or the instrumental piano album *Ferrante & Teicher Play The Carpenters Songbook*, both from 1975. In contrast, this tribute album is notable for assembling 14 artists from the 1990s alternative-

rock scene, including Redd Kross, Grant Lee Buffalo and American Music Club. Released on A&M as part of the 25th-anniversary celebrations, the project was overseen by producer Matt Wallace (Faith No More and The Replacements) and music journalist David Konjoyan, friends who shared a genuine affection for the Carpenters' music. The project was no doubt inspired by the trend of tribute albums at that time, where artists like Lou Reed, Nick Cave, Elton John and Kate Bush reinterpreted the music of people like Cole Porter, George Gershwin and Leonard Cohen.

As a precursor to this project, in 1987, underground film director Todd Haynes made an irreverent art film of Karen Carpenter's life using Barbie dolls, and Sonic Youth recorded 'Tunic (Song for Karen)' on their 1990 album *Goo*.

Back in 1983, California's Circle Jerks had given 'Close To You' a punk makeover on their *Golden Shower of Hits* album. The Cranberries give a more-considered interpretation on this album, while Matthew Sweet's version of 'Let Me Be the One' is a standout, featuring Richard on keyboards and backing vocals. Other artists move further away from the Carpenters' sound, often using distortion and noise, like Dutch band Bettie Serveert's take on 'For All We Know'.

Fittingly, three of the bands feature female drummers, and Babes in Toyland drummer Lori Barbero also sings lead on their version of 'Calling Occupants Of Interplanetary Craft'. Other artists considered for the project were Smashing Pumpkins, Stone Temple Pilots, and Paul Westerberg of the Replacements.

The album was released on CD and as a set of 7" singles, with sleeves featuring close-ups of the duo's faces. The front cover was a cartoon of the pair with big eyes, in the style of kitsch painter Margaret Keane.

Love Songs (1997)

Aimed at the Japan and Hong Kong markets, *22 Hits of The Carpenters* appeared in 1995, reaching three in Japan, and becoming the duo's biggest seller there, leading to renewed interest in the duo.

In 1997, *Reader's Digest* released the 3-CD set *Their Greatest Hits and Finest Performances*, which included the full-length live Bacharach/David medley for the first time on a non-Japan release. It also included a remix of 'Medley' from *Now And Then* with the sound effects and DJ voice removed.

The success of these compilations is thought to have caused A&M UK to release *Love Songs* in 1997, with 20 tracks spanning the group's career. The collection became a popular seller in the States, where it stayed on the charts for six months, helped by new documentaries on PBS, A&E and VH1. The selection was later repackaged to match the Carpenters' *Gold* cover design.

30th Anniversary Collector's Edition (1998)

A CD box set of 11 studio albums (minus the Christmas releases) was issued exclusively for collectors in Japan. Each CD was packaged in a miniature reproduction of the album sleeve. There was also a booklet with notes from Richard, rare photos, and a black handkerchief bearing the Carpenters' logo. The 2003 reissue as the *35th Anniversary Collector's Edition* included the Christmas albums. Reissued again in 2009 as the *40th Anniversary Collector's Edition,* each album appeared in the SHM-CD (Super High Material) format, and came with its own individual booklet. The set also included the compilations *As Time Goes By* and *Sweet Sixteen*. The final ingredient was The Carpenters *Gold* DVD.

The Singles 1969-1981 (2000)

Released in Asia and other territories in 1999, this compilation arrived in the US in 2000, with an Annie Leibowitz cover portrait from the 1974 *Rolling Stone* shoot. Although the title suggests a comprehensive round-up, there are just 20 of the 30 US singles released in the given period. Fans in Japan had to wait till 2006 before the *Japanese Single Box* was issued, containing 33 3" mini-CDs replicating the Japanese singles. The US singles were collated on three CDs in 2015 as *The Complete Singles,* containing every A and B side, with only a couple of album tracks slipping through.

Bookending the collection are two versions of 'For All We Know'. The closing 'Reprise' comes from the 1972 TV show *The Special London Bridge Special* starring Tom Jones. The track lasts less than a minute, and has Karen singing with an orchestra, used in the special to accompany a ballet sequence featuring Rudolph Nureyev and Merle Park. In addition, there's a new piano segue linking 'I Won't Last a Day Without You' to 'Close To You'.

In 2004, the compilation was re-released on SA-CD with three layers: standard CD, SA-CD stereo and a 5.1 surround mix, remixed by Richard and Grammy-winning engineer/producer Al Schmitt, who'd worked with Ray Charles, Frank Sinatra, Steely Dan and Paul McCartney.

Gold (2000)

Not to be confused with the earlier *A&M Gold Series* compilations, this European release contained 20 of their best singles, mostly in remixed form. The cover was reminiscent of the 1992 compilation *Abba Gold*.

Gold was issued in Japan with 21 tracks in 2001. It was released in the US in 2004, subtitled *35th Anniversary Edition,* comprising two CDs with a total of 40 songs. The US was the first reissue to include the single mix of 'Solitaire', and also a new piano link between 'Top Of The World' and 'Maybe It's You'.

Gold was reissued in the UK in 2005, and the DVD *Gold: Greatest Hits* was released in 2002.

As Time Goes By (2001)

This rarities compilation was first released in Japan in 2001, then elsewhere in 2004. Reaching back to early 1967 demos of 'Nowhere Man' and 'California

Dreamin", the collection mostly focuses on TV broadcasts, ranging from the 1971 *Live at the BBC* concert to their final special *Music Music Music* in 1980. The cover photo comes from the 1974 *Rolling Stone* shoot. All tracks are discussed in the Related Tracks sections in earlier chapters.

40/40 (2009)
This two-CD best-of has 40 tracks and was released for the duo's 40th anniversary, reaching number two in Norway, and three in Japan. The single CD edition *20/20* was released in Japan the same year.

The Nation's Favourite Carpenters Songs (2016)
UK network ITV broadcast *The Nation's Favourite Carpenters Song* on 3 September 2016, presenting the results of a UK vote to find the group's 20 best-loved songs. The show included new interviews with Richard, John Bettis, Paul Williams, Petula Clark and Herb Alpert, amongst others. Other artists featured in this series of programmes included Abba, The Beatles, The Bee Gees and Elvis Presley.

The top three Carpenters songs in the poll were 'Top Of The World', 'We've Only Just Begun' and 'Please Mr. Postman'. The compilation was issued to coincide with the programme, with the 20 songs in chronological order, as opposed to following the order of the poll results.

'Goodbye To Love' includes the original studio count-in, while 'I Won't Last A Day Without You' ends with the extended piano outro from *Singles 1969-1981*, though this is no longer linked to 'Goodbye To Love'. The album reached two in the UK.

Classic Carpenters – Dami Im (2016)
South Korean-born Australian artist Dami Im was a winner of *X Factor Australia* in 2013. Her album of Carpenters' covers contained 11 of their biggest hits. Im explained that it wasn't her intention to copy Karen's singing style, but rather to interpret the melodies through her own voice.

Most of the songs have a contemporary R&B ballad feel, though some familiar elements are retained, such as the iconic piano intro of 'Close To You' and the brass hits of 'We've Only Just Begun'.

The album reached 3 in Australia and 23 in South Korea, though Im has since distanced herself from the release, stating it was Sony's decision to record cover versions when she wanted to record her own original songs.

A Tribute To The Carpenters – Carla Williams (2022)
Alabama-based country singer Carla Williams teamed up with legendary singer-songwriter/producer Michael Omartian to record this collection of 15 songs, including 'Rainbow Connection' and 'Merry Christmas, Darling'. Williams had often been told how much her voice sounded like Karen's, which led her to record this tribute. Guest musicians include Sir Cliff Richard

on 'Hurting Each Other', Toto's Steve Lukather playing the guitar solo on 'Goodbye To Love', and Chicago's Bill Champlin and Jeff Coffey contributing innovative backing vocals to 'We've Only Just Begun'. Strings were recorded at Abbey Road.

Solo Albums and Reinterpretations

Time (1987)

Having arranged, sung backing vocals and played keyboards on Smokey Robinson's 1986 album *Smoke Signals*, Richard's first solo album was released in October 1987, boldly embracing a contemporary sound reminiscent in places of Chicago's 1982 ballad 'Hard to Say I'm Sorry' and Starship's 1985 hit 'We Built This City'.

Richard sings lead on six tracks, with the others sung by guest vocalists, including Dusty Springfield on the lead single 'Something in Your Eyes', which reached two on the Adult Contemporary chart. Dionne Warwick sings 'In Time Alone'. Both of those songs were originally written for Karen to sing on *Voice Of The Heart*. Newcomer Scott Grimes (just 15 at the time) sings 'That's What I Believe'. 'When Time Was All We Had' is dedicated to Karen, featuring dazzling multitracked vocal harmonies by Richard, and an emotional flugelhorn solo from Herb Alpert. The title track is an instrumental and was released as a promotional single in the US.

Richard wrote the songs with a variety of people, including Tim Rice, Cynthia Weil, Richard Marx and, of course, John Bettis. Other familiar musicians include Tony Peluso, Joe Osborn, and percussionist Paulinho Da Costa, who'd appeared on *Made In America* and *Voice Of The Heart*.

The album jacket shows Richard leaning against his red 1962 Thunderbird Roadster, with his name designed in a logo resembling the vehicle's shiny chrome lettering.

Karen Carpenter (1996)

Karen had been waiting for a chance to record a solo album, and the opportunity arose in early 1979 when the band was put on hold to give Richard time to recover from his addiction. A&M's Alpert and Moss were initially supportive, and suggested producer Phil Ramone, who'd won Grammys for his work with Paul Simon and Billy Joel.

When Ramone asked Karen what kind of music she wanted to record, straight away she mentioned disco-queen Donna Summer, regardless of Richard's advice to avoid disco. Ramone, therefore, brought in Rod Temperton – former Heatwave member and writer of their hit 'Boogie Nights'. Around this time, Temperton also placed songs with Michael Jackson, and actually offered Karen early versions of 'Off the Wall' and 'Rock With You', which she turned down. Ramone took Karen to visit Jackson in the studio as he recorded 'Get on the Floor' for the *Off the Wall* album. Jackson had written the song with bass player Louis Johnson, who also played on Karen's album. Keyboardist Greg Phillinganes also played on both albums.

Other songwriters included John Farrar – composer/producer for Olivia Newton-John and Chicago's Peter Cetera. Karen also recorded a version of Paul Simon's hit 'Still Crazy After All These Years'. Ramone recruited a range of musicians, including jazz legends Bob James and Michael Brecker, renowned session drummer Steve Gadd and percussionist Airto Moreira. Ramone also brought in Billy Joel guitarist Russell Javors, who played on three songs.

Aside from disco, Karen also recorded in country, blues and rock. She was clearly ready to try something new, even when the songs contained more overtly sexual lyrics than anything she had recorded with the Carpenters. The closest to a Carpenters' song was the ballad 'Make Believe It's Your First Time', and the duo re-recorded this song for *Voice Of The Heart*.

Recording began in early May 1979 at Ramone's A&R Studios in New York. 21 tracks were recorded and the sessions were completed by January 1980. The solo album was announced to fans through the band's newsletter, and A&M began a promotional campaign, assigning the album a catalogue number and planning a spring release. Ramone held a playback of 11 songs for A&M executives, at his studio, and the album was well-received. But it was met with an entirely different reception on the West Coast, where it was said to lack hit material and was in need of further work. Moreover, with titles like 'Making Love in the Afternoon', it was considered too great a departure from the Carpenters' image to market to their fans easily. To her great disappointment, Karen found herself agreeing to put the album aside. In May 1980, a *Billboard* article stated she'd elected to shelve her solo album to concentrate on the Carpenters.

The album remained unheard until its release in 1996 at the request of fans. It arrived with a cover portrait by fashion photographer Claude Mougin, who'd also shot cover photos for Olivia Newton-John, Carole Bayer Sager and Airto Moreira. The album contained 11 songs in the same mixes Karen had approved for release in 1980. A 12th song – 'Last One Singin' the Blues' – was included as a bonus, with Karen's instructions to the band left in at the start and middle of the song. By the time of release, seven of the songs had already appeared in some form on *Voice Of The Heart*, *Lovelines* and *From the Top*. Of the 21 songs recorded, nine have yet to be released, though, around 1996, an A&M employee leaked rough mixes that have since found their way onto the internet. These include Martha and the Vandellas 1967 hit 'Jimmy Mack', and Paul Simon's 'I Do It for Your Love'. Selected songs from this album are discussed in the Related Tracks section of this book.

Richard Carpenter: Pianist, Arranger, Composer, Conductor (1998)

Richard released this mainly instrumental album partly at the suggestion of his friend, musician and psychologist Daniel J. Levitin, and partly at the request of Japanese fans. The album title acknowledges Richard's various musical skills and contributions to the Carpenters. Of course, the list in the title could also have included 'producer' and 'singer', since Richard produced this album, and his backing vocals appear at the end of the track 'Time'.

There are 14 tracks, including a medley of seven songs. The set mixes classic Carpenters tracks with newer compositions, such as the opening

'Prelude': a short piece in a light classical style. 'Time' is a remix of the 1987 recording on Richard's first solo album, while 'All Those Years Ago' was written for Canadian singer/actress Véronique Béliveau in 1989 when Richard produced her album *Véronique.* Richard also produced Japanese artist Akiko's 1988 album *City of Angels* and Scott Grimes' 1990 solo album. 'Karen's Theme' was a melody written for the 1989 TV movie *The Karen Carpenter Story*, and was given an expanded arrangement here.

Classic Carpenters songs receive something of a makeover here, as 'Yesterday Once More' is played to a country rhythm, and 'Sing' is embellished with baroque features. Instrumental versions of 'Look to Your Dreams' and 'Someday' sound especially poignant, and it is hard not to imagine Karen singing it. She does, in fact, appear, as her original drum track for 'Flat Baroque' is used on the re-recorded version. Karen is also credited with vocals on 'Sandy', though it's difficult to pick out her voice amongst the O.K. Chorale choir. Earle Dumler, Tony Peluso, Joe Osborn and Tommy Morgan all make return appearances. Recordings took place at Capitol Studios in Los Angeles.

While some critics dismissed the album as 'elevator music', it presents a different take on some of the duo's best-known tunes. 'Karen's Theme' was released as a single but failed to chart. The album was dedicated to the duo's mother, Agnes Carpenter, who'd passed away in October 1996.

Carpenters With The Royal Philharmonic Orchestra (2018)

For this album, Richard collaborated with the Royal Philharmonic Orchestra on updates of 17 Carpenters songs, combining old and new recordings. The orchestra was established in the 1940s with the royal approval of King George VI and later Queen Elizabeth II. Though mainly dedicated to classical music, the orchestra recorded a version of Mike Oldfield's *Tubular Bells* in the 1970s, and the 1980s *Hooked on Classics* albums. Prior to the Carpenters project, the RPO had added orchestral parts to classic recordings by Buddy Holly, Elvis Presley, Roy Orbison, Aretha Franklin and The Beach Boys.

The project began when the orchestra invited Richard to collaborate. Carpenters remixes were completed ahead of the orchestra sessions. Thanks to digital editing, a few out-of-tune instruments were pitch-corrected, not to mention the removal of mouth sounds on Karen's vocals and a creaky piano pedal on 'Close To You'. Furthermore, this allowed for tempo correction on songs where the band had gotten faster from the start to the end of the recording.

With preparations complete, Richard travelled to London to conduct the musicians at Abbey Road Studio Two. The project was an opportunity for Richard to write new parts for several songs, such as the Beatlesque piccolo trumpet on 'Goodbye To Love' and 'Baby It's You'. New Spanish guitar lines were also added to 'Superstar' for the line 'Your guitar, it sounds so sweet and clear'.

Having originally recorded with small ensembles of ten violins, three violas and three celli, Richard now had 40 violins in an 80-piece orchestra. Returning to L.A., Richard transported his own Steinway piano to Capitol Studios for additional overdubs.

'Please Mr. Postman' was an exclusive bonus track for the Japanese edition and a CD available at Target stores in the US. In this recording, the band instruments drop out for a verse, and the strings take over. A single featuring 'Ticket To Ride', 'Yesterday Once More' and 'Merry Christmas, Darling' was released around the same time as the album.

Richard Carpenter's Piano Songbook (2021)

For his third album, revisiting Carpenters songs, Richard simply played the piano. The idea came in 2018 when he gave an impromptu piano performance of 'I Need to Be in Love' at a promotional event for the RPO album. In the audience was Rachel Holmberg – Senior Head of A&R for Decca Records – who suggested Richard record an album of Carpenters piano solos for the label.

There are 12 selections, comprising well-known singles along with 'Rainbow Connection'. The opening medley combines 'Sing', 'Goodbye To Love', 'Eve' and 'Rainy Days And Mondays'. Some pieces feature chord variations and new rhythms, while others are more subtly restyled with occasional ornamentation. In a promo video for the album, Richard said, 'The hardest part was making (the songs) honest and acceptable as solo piano pieces, without getting too showy'. The rare 'Eve' was also interpreted. Other novelties include withholding the iconic piano introduction of 'Close To You' until the song's coda, while 'Top Of The World' begins with the same introduction heard on the *Pianist, Composer, Arranger, Conductor* album.

The album was released on vinyl, CD and digital in late 2021 in Japan, and January 2022 in the US. Three singles were released: '(They Long To Be) Close To You' in October 2021, 'Yesterday Once More' in November 2021, and 'We've Only Just Begun' in December 2021, none of which charted. The album was recorded at Nest Studios in Woodland Hills, California, and the colourful cover art contains pictorial references to several of the songs.

On Karen's Voice

Karen Carpenter interviewed by Ray Coleman, *Melody Maker* (1975):

I never really discovered the voice that you know now, the low one, until later, when I was 16. I used to sing in this upper voice, and I didn't like it. I was uncomfortable, so I think I would tend to shy away from it because I didn't think I was that good.

Label manager and artist Herb Alpert, interviewed by Ray Coleman:

It had so much presence ... It felt like her voice was on the couch like she was sitting next to me. It was full and round, and it was ... amazing.

Road manager Paul White, interviewed by Ray Coleman:

She used to hit the notes like radar. Some singers hit them a little under, and slide up or down. Karen was pure.

Biographer Ray Coleman:

As Roger Young, their engineer, points out, because Karen sang very softly – very close to the microphone by habit – the intense presence of her voice was accentuated.

Songwriter and producer Nicky Chinn, interviewed by Lucy O'Brien:

I've listened closely, and you can hear the pain. Karen didn't just sing a song; she understood every word, and she put her emotion into it. And you can hear the pain in her voice very, very often, because she was a girl in pain.

Richard Carpenter, interviewed by Ray Coleman:

Karen had the uncanny ability to sing lyrics about-which she had no experience, and make them sound like she'd lived every damned experience! She was only 21 years old when she sang 'Rainy Days And Mondays', and she sounds way beyond her years.

Richard Carpenter, from the Carpenters' official website *Fans Ask... ... Richard Answers* page:

Q: How could you tell that a song was tailor-made for Karen?
A: It's really where it would dwell in a particular register; not spend too much of its time upstairs, because Karen had such a marvellous sound in

the lower reaches of her voice. How words sing – As, Os and Us are better sounds than Es and Is. That's one of many reasons why 'Superstar' worked so well for Karen – it's low, it has 'long ago', 'far away', 'second show', 'it's just the radio', it's absolutely perfect. Again, we were family, and a lot of this was intuitive. It would have a nice melody, and I knew Karen's voice would give me chills singing it.

Selected Bibliography

Carpenters Complete (CPP Belwin, Inc., 1985)
Cidoni L. M., May C., *Carpenters: The Musical Legacy* (Princeton Architectural Press, 2021)
Coleman R., *The Carpenters: The Untold Story* (Boxtree, 1994)
Halstead C., *Carpenters: All the Top 40 Hits* (2015. Reprint, Amazon, 2022)
O'Brien L., *Lead Sister: The Story of Karen Carpenter* (Nine Eight Books, 2023)
Schmidt R. L., *Little Girl Blue: The Life of Karen Carpenter* (Omnibus Press, 2012)
Schmidt R. L., *Carpenters: An Illustrated Discography* (Mascot Books, 2019)
Tobler J., *The Complete Guide to the Music of The Carpenters* (Omnibus, 1998)

Selected Online Resources

Carpenters Album Covers: http://vinylalbumcovers.com/
Carpenters Avenue: https://carponline.proboards.com/
Carpenters Complete Recording Resource: https://carpenters.amcorner.com/
Carpenters Official Website: https://www.richardandkarencarpenter.com/
Karen Carpenter's Vocal Range: https://therangeplanet.proboards.com/

Laura Nyro - *on track*
every album, every song

Philip Ward
Paperback
144 pages
40 colour photographs
978-1-78951-182-5
£15.99
$22.95

Every album and every song by this influential singer-songwriter.

Laura Nyro (1947-1997) was one of the most significant figures to emerge from the singer-songwriter boom of the 1960s. She first came to attention when her songs were hits for Barbra Streisand, The Fifth Dimension, Peter, Paul and Mary, and others. But it was on her own recordings that she imprinted her vibrant personality. With albums like *Eli And The Thirteenth Confession* and *New York Tendaberry* she mixed the sounds of soul, pop, jazz and Broadway to fashion autobiographical songs that earned her a fanatical following and influenced a generation of music-makers. In later life her preoccupations shifted from the self to embrace public causes such as feminism, animal rights and ecology – the music grew mellower, but her genius was undimmed.

This book examines her entire studio career from 1967's *More Than A New Discovery* to the posthumous *Angel In The Dark* release of 2001. Also surveyed are the many live albums that preserve her charismatic stage presence. With analysis of her teasing, poetic lyrics and unique vocal and harmonic style, this is the first-ever study to concentrate on Laura Nyro's music and how she created it. Elton John idolised her; Joni Mitchell declared her 'a complete original'. Here's why

Misty - The Music of Johnny Mathis
Foreword by Johnny Mathis

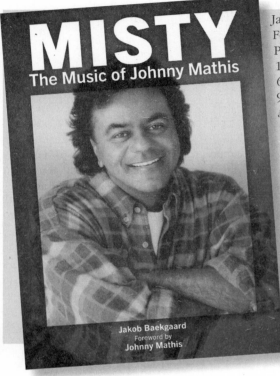

Jakob Baekgaard
Foreword by Johnny Mathis
Paperback
192 pages
60 colour photographs
978-1-78951-247-1
£17.99
$24.95

The musical life of this famed jazz/soul singer.

Few singers have been able to change with the times like Johnny Mathis. Although his fame rests on his massive popularity in the 50s and 60s when he competed with Elvis and Frank Sinatra and outsold almost anyone, Mathis has remained relevant through the decades and no other crooner is as technically skilled or able to cover multiple genres so convincingly. Jazz, soul, disco, country, classic and contemporary pop, Mathis has adapted his impressive vocal range to all kinds of music and transgressed the stereotype of what a male voice is supposed to sound like.

The longest-running artist on Columbia, he has been recognized by the record industry with The Recording Academy Lifetime Achievement Award and three recordings in the Grammy Hall of Fame, but so far, there hasn't been an exhaustive examination of his complete recordings in book form. Authorized by Mathis and including fresh insights from himself as well as his producers and arrangers, Misty: The Music of Johnny Mathis, rights that wrong. With detailed discussions of the records and a discography, the book traces Mathis's musical journey from the past to the present and includes a wealth of photos and album scans from his own archive. It's the ideal companion for fans and new listeners interested in exploring one of the most prominent voices in American music.

On Track series
Allman Brothers Band – Andrew Wild 978-1-78952-252-5
Tori Amos – Lisa Torem 978-1-78952-142-9
Aphex Twin – Beau Waddell 978-1-78952-267-9
Asia – Peter Braidis 978-1-78952-099-6
Badfinger – Robert Day-Webb 978-1-878952-176-4
Barclay James Harvest – Keith and Monica Domone 978-1-78952-067-5
Beck – Arthur Lizie 978-1-78952-258-7
The Beatles – Andrew Wild 978-1-78952-009-5
The Beatles Solo 1969-1980 – Andrew Wild 978-1-78952-030-9
Blue Oyster Cult – Jacob Holm-Lupo 978-1-78952-007-1
Blur – Matt Bishop 978-178952-164-1
Marc Bolan and T.Rex – Peter Gallagher 978-1-78952-124-5
Kate Bush – Bill Thomas 978-1-78952-097-2
Camel – Hamish Kuzminski 978-1-78952-040-8
Captain Beefheart – Opher Goodwin 978-1-78952-235-8
Caravan – Andy Boot 978-1-78952-127-6
Cardiacs – Eric Benac 978-1-78952-131-3
Nick Cave and The Bad Seeds – Dominic Sanderson 978-1-78952-240-2
Eric Clapton Solo – Andrew Wild 978-1-78952-141-2
The Clash – Nick Assirati 978-1-78952-077-4
Elvis Costello and The Attractions – Georg Purvis 978-1-78952-129-0
Crosby, Stills and Nash – Andrew Wild 978-1-78952-039-2
Creedence Clearwater Revival – Tony Thompson 978-178952-237-2
The Damned – Morgan Brown 978-1-78952-136-8
Deep Purple and Rainbow 1968-79 – Steve Pilkington 978-1-78952-002-6
Dire Straits – Andrew Wild 978-1-78952-044-6
The Doors – Tony Thompson 978-1-78952-137-5
Dream Theater – Jordan Blum 978-1-78952-050-7
Eagles – John Van der Kiste 978-1-78952-260-0
Earth, Wind and Fire – Bud Wilkins 978-1-78952-272-3
Electric Light Orchestra – Barry Delve 978-1-78952-152-8
Emerson Lake and Palmer – Mike Goode 978-1-78952-000-2
Fairport Convention – Kevan Furbank 978-1-78952-051-4
Peter Gabriel – Graeme Scarfe 978-1-78952-138-2
Genesis – Stuart MacFarlane 978-1-78952-005-7
Gentle Giant – Gary Steel 978-1-78952-058-3
Gong – Kevan Furbank 978-1-78952-082-8
Green Day – William E. Spevack 978-1-78952-261-7
Hall and Oates – Ian Abrahams 978-1-78952-167-2
Hawkwind – Duncan Harris 978-1-78952-052-1
Peter Hammill – Richard Rees Jones 978-1-78952-163-4
Roy Harper – Opher Goodwin 978-1-78952-130-6

Jimi Hendrix – Emma Stott 978-1-78952-175-7
The Hollies – Andrew Darlington 978-1-78952-159-7
Horslips – Richard James 978-1-78952-263-1
The Human League and The Sheffield Scene –
Andrew Darlington 978-1-78952-186-3
The Incredible String Band – Tim Moon 978-1-78952-107-8
Iron Maiden – Steve Pilkington 978-1-78952-061-3
Joe Jackson – Richard James 978-1-78952-189-4
Jefferson Airplane – Richard Butterworth 978-1-78952-143-6
Jethro Tull – Jordan Blum 978-1-78952-016-3
Elton John in the 1970s – Peter Kearns 978-1-78952-034-7
Billy Joel – Lisa Torem 978-1-78952-183-2
Judas Priest – John Tucker 978-1-78952-018-7
Kansas – Kevin Cummings 978-1-78952-057-6
The Kinks – Martin Hutchinson 978-1-78952-172-6
Korn – Matt Karpe 978-1-78952-153-5
Led Zeppelin – Steve Pilkington 978-1-78952-151-1
Level 42 – Matt Philips 978-1-78952-102-3
Little Feat – Georg Purvis - 978-1-78952-168-9
Aimee Mann – Jez Rowden 978-1-78952-036-1
Joni Mitchell – Peter Kearns 978-1-78952-081-1
The Moody Blues – Geoffrey Feakes 978-1-78952-042-2
Motorhead – Duncan Harris 978-1-78952-173-3
Nektar – Scott Meze – 978-1-78952-257-0
New Order – Dennis Remmer – 978-1-78952-249-5
Nightwish – Simon McMurdo – 978-1-78952-270-9
Laura Nyro – Philip Ward 978-1-78952-182-5
Mike Oldfield – Ryan Yard 978-1-78952-060-6
Opeth – Jordan Blum 978-1-78-952-166-5
Pearl Jam – Ben L. Connor 978-1-78952-188-7
Tom Petty – Richard James 978-1-78952-128-3
Pink Floyd – Richard Butterworth 978-1-78952-242-6
The Police – Pete Braidis 978-1-78952-158-0
Porcupine Tree – Nick Holmes 978-1-78952-144-3
Queen – Andrew Wild 978-1-78952-003-3
Radiohead – William Allen 978-1-78952-149-8
Rancid – Paul Matts 989-1-78952-187-0
Renaissance – David Detmer 978-1-78952-062-0
REO Speedwagon – Jim Romag 978-1-78952-262-4
The Rolling Stones 1963-80 – Steve Pilkington 978-1-78952-017-0
The Smiths and Morrissey – Tommy Gunnarsson 978-1-78952-140-5
Spirit – Rev. Keith A. Gordon – 978-1-78952- 248-8
Stackridge – Alan Draper 978-1-78952-232-7

Status Quo the Frantic Four Years – Richard James 978-1-78952-160-3
Steely Dan – Jez Rowden 978-1-78952-043-9
Steve Hackett – Geoffrey Feakes 978-1-78952-098-9
Tears For Fears – Paul Clark - 978-178952-238-9
Thin Lizzy – Graeme Stroud 978-1-78952-064-4
Tool – Matt Karpe 978-1-78952-234-1
Toto – Jacob Holm-Lupo 978-1-78952-019-4
U2 – Eoghan Lyng 978-1-78952-078-1
UFO – Richard James 978-1-78952-073-6
Van Der Graaf Generator – Dan Coffey 978-1-78952-031-6
Van Halen – Morgan Brown – 9781-78952-256-3
The Who – Geoffrey Feakes 978-1-78952-076-7
Roy Wood and the Move – James R Turner 978-1-78952-008-8
Yes – Stephen Lambe 978-1-78952-001-9
Frank Zappa 1966 to 1979 – Eric Benac 978-1-78952-033-0
Warren Zevon – Peter Gallagher 978-1-78952-170-2
10CC – Peter Kearns 978-1-78952-054-5

Decades Series
The Bee Gees in the 1960s – Andrew Mon Hughes et al 978-1-78952-148-1
The Bee Gees in the 1970s – Andrew Mon Hughes et al 978-1-78952-179-5
Black Sabbath in the 1970s – Chris Sutton 978-1-78952-171-9
Britpop – Peter Richard Adams and Matt Pooler 978-1-78952-169-6
Phil Collins in the 1980s – Andrew Wild 978-1-78952-185-6
Alice Cooper in the 1970s – Chris Sutton 978-1-78952-104-7
Alice Cooper in the 1980s – Chris Sutton 978-1-78952-259-4
Curved Air in the 1970s – Laura Shenton 978-1-78952-069-9
Donovan in the 1960s – Jeff Fitzgerald 978-1-78952-233-4
Bob Dylan in the 1980s – Don Klees 978-1-78952-157-3
Brian Eno in the 1970s – Gary Parsons 978-1-78952-239-6
Faith No More in the 1990s – Matt Karpe 978-1-78952-250-1
Fleetwood Mac in the 1970s – Andrew Wild 978-1-78952-105-4
Fleetwood Mac in the 1980s – Don Klees 978-178952-254-9
Focus in the 1970s – Stephen Lambe 978-1-78952-079-8
Free and Bad Company in the 1970s – John Van der Kiste 978-1-78952-178-8
Genesis in the 1970s – Bill Thomas 978178952-146-7
George Harrison in the 1970s – Eoghan Lyng 978-1-78952-174-0
Kiss in the 1970s – Peter Gallagher 978-1-78952-246-4
Manfred Mann's Earth Band in the 1970s – John Van der Kiste 978178952-243-3
Marillion in the 1980s – Nathaniel Webb 978-1-78952-065-1
Van Morrison in the 1970s – Peter Childs - 978-1-78952-241-9
Mott the Hoople and Ian Hunter in the 1970s –
John Van der Kiste 978-1-78-952-162-7

Pink Floyd In The 1970s – Georg Purvis 978-1-78952-072-9
Suzi Quatro in the 1970s – Darren Johnson 978-1-78952-236-5
Queen in the 1970s – James Griffiths 978-1-78952-265-5
Roxy Music in the 1970s – Dave Thompson 978-1-78952-180-1
Slade in the 1970s – Darren Johnson 978-1-78952-268-6
Status Quo in the 1980s – Greg Harper 978-1-78952-244-0
Tangerine Dream in the 1970s – Stephen Palmer 978-1-78952-161-0
The Sweet in the 1970s – Darren Johnson 978-1-78952-139-9
Uriah Heep in the 1970s – Steve Pilkington 978-1-78952-103-0
Van der Graaf Generator in the 1970s – Steve Pilkington 978-1-78952-245-7
Rick Wakeman in the 1970s – Geoffrey Feakes 978-1-78952-264-8
Yes in the 1980s – Stephen Lambe with David Watkinson 978-1-78952-125-2

On Screen series
Carry On... – Stephen Lambe 978-1-78952-004-0
David Cronenberg – Patrick Chapman 978-1-78952-071-2
Doctor Who: The David Tennant Years – Jamie Hailstone 978-1-78952-066-8
James Bond – Andrew Wild 978-1-78952-010-1
Monty Python – Steve Pilkington 978-1-78952-047-7
Seinfeld Seasons 1 to 5 – Stephen Lambe 978-1-78952-012-5

Other Books
1967: A Year In Psychedelic Rock 978-1-78952-155-9
1970: A Year In Rock – John Van der Kiste 978-1-78952-147-4
1973: The Golden Year of Progressive Rock 978-1-78952-165-8
Babysitting A Band On The Rocks – G.D. Praetorius 978-1-78952-106-1
Eric Clapton Sessions – Andrew Wild 978-1-78952-177-1
Derek Taylor: For Your Radioactive Children –
Andrew Darlington 978-1-78952-038-5
The Golden Road: The Recording History of The Grateful Dead – John Kilbride 978-1-78952-156-6
Iggy and The Stooges On Stage 1967-1974 – Per Nilsen 978-1-78952-101-6
Jon Anderson and the Warriors – the road to Yes –
David Watkinson 978-1-78952-059-0
Magic: The David Paton Story – David Paton 978-1-78952-266-2
Misty: The Music of Johnny Mathis – Jakob Baekgaard 978-1-78952-247-1
Nu Metal: A Definitive Guide – Matt Karpe 978-1-78952-063-7
Tommy Bolin: In and Out of Deep Purple – Laura Shenton 978-1-78952-070-5
Maximum Darkness – Deke Leonard 978-1-78952-048-4
The Twang Dynasty – Deke Leonard 978-1-78952-049-1

and many more to come!

Would you like to write for Sonicbond Publishing?

At Sonicbond Publishing we are always on the look-out for authors, particularly for our two main series:

On Track. Mixing fact with in depth analysis, the On Track series examines the work of a particular musical artist or group. All genres are considered from easy listening and jazz to 60s soul to 90s pop, via rock and metal.

On Screen. This series looks at the world of film and television. Subjects considered include directors, actors and writers, as well as entire television and film series. As with the On Track series, we balance fact with analysis.

While professional writing experience would, of course, be an advantage the most important qualification is to have real enthusiasm and knowledge of your subject. First-time authors are welcomed, but the ability to write well in English is essential.

Sonicbond Publishing has distribution throughout Europe and North America, and all books are also published in E-book form. Authors will be paid a royalty based on sales of their book.

Further details are available from www.sonicbondpublishing.co.uk. To contact us, complete the contact form there or
email info@sonicbondpublishing.co.uk